CW00428989

Where Are They Now?

Where Are They Now?

POP & ROCK

Andy Pringle

TWO HEADS
PUBLISHING

First published in 1997 by
Two Heads Publishing
9 Whitehall Park
London N19 3TS

© *Andy Pringle* 1997

ISBN 1897850237

Cover & book design by Lance Bellers
Printed in the UK by Biddles, Guildford

Thanks to

ABBA Fan Club; Alan Pearce; Alan Williams; Band 6 – Monkees Official UK Fan Club;
Barry Whitwam Assocs; Black Sabbath Appreciation Society; Bobby Vee
Connection; Brenda Lee Fan Club; Brian Poole; Charles Frewin; Lance Bellers;
Q Magazine; Chris Cornish, Caterbridge Ltd; Craig Monk; Cos Comino; Darlings
Of Wapping Wharf Launderette; Dave Jewell; David Clayton; Friends of Mike
Berry; Gay Wiggins; Geoff Downes; Geoff Webb; Graham Fenton; Guy Mitchell
Appreciation Society; Impressions (ELP); Jacky Cain; John Holman; John Van Der
Kist; Keep On Running (Dexys); Ken Coombes; Mark Hadley Photography, (G
Giltrap); Mike Pender's Searchers Fan Club; Miriam Bruinsuma; Mungo Jerry
International Fan Club; Naked Eye (The Who); Nut Inc (Madness); Queen Fan Club;
Ron Ellis; Shine On (Procol Harum); Staff at Shooters Bar & Diner, Windsor; Martyn
Hanson (ELP); Tom Hammond; Uriah Heep Appreciation Society; But most of all to
Geraldine, Hannah and Sarah-Jayne for putting up with another flight of fancy!

Author's Note

Thank you for opening this book an even bigger than you if you bought it yourself!). By doing so you have proved that I am not alone in being intrigued to find out what happened to the artists who provided the musical backdrop to our formative years.

If you are looking for a 'definitive' guide to pop and rock history – please look a little further along the bookshelves, where you will find dozens of far more suitable tomes (they are generally thicker with much smaller print). According to the latest 'Guinness Book of Hit Singles' there have been over 4,000 acts to appear in the singles charts since their inception in 1952, making it an impossible and impracticable task to include everyone – so please forgive me if your favourite has been missed.

Who would you include or exclude? The decision is not helped by the fact that the vast majority of groups from the past twenty five years still exist in name, some with full original membership, others with none at all. Other stars have stood the test of time and are still thriving today. Please be assured that because someone has been mentioned, it is not meant to imply that they are past their best, or worst still, forgotten. Many performers have stronger support today than in their supposed heyday and many are certainly earning far more money!

Not being a historian or journalist, but merely someone who likes music, I naively assumed that most showbiz types are extroverted and grateful for any extra free publicity on offer. How wrong can you be! While many artists, managers, agents and fan clubs were most co-operative, there were plenty more who either were protective (understandable, maybe), awkward (unnecessary) or just rude (unforgivable).

You would be amazed at how often my innocent enquiry met with surprise that

an artist should even be considered for inclusion in such a book (even if they had been out of the charts for as much as a quarter of a century!). Maybe the job would have been easier if I had followed Russ Conway's advice and re-titled the book 'Where They Are Now !'

I must admit I did also invite trouble for myself. In an attempt to minimise the risk of any damage to sensitive egos, I r-worded my written request for information to suggest that while I understood that .... was still a big star (creeping), there is a genuine interest in finding out about artists who may not have had recent chart presence. Among the new batch of respondents were David Essex's management who pointed out that their client was at that time riding high in the album charts therefore prompting their own question 'WHERE ARE YOU NOW ?' Quite.

Despite all the hurdles, compiling this book was great fun and would not have been possible without the help of hundreds of people who also presumably also risked marital wrath to find out 'Where Are They Now ?' On their behalf, I sincerely hope that you enjoy reading the answers as much as I enjoyed finding them!

Andy Pringle

Abba

ABBA

The audience that gathered in Brighton to enjoy the 1974 Eurovision Song Contest could have had no idea that they would be witnessing the launch one of the biggest selling acts of all time. Their winning song Waterloo itself old over five million copies and at one stage their record company, Polar, was the most successful company in Sweden even surpassing motor giants Volvo. In 1993, long after the group and their respective marriages had long gone, the band were still Sweden's bestselling recording artists.

The group had gone their separate ways in 1982 when the two female singers Agnetha Faltskog (the blonde), and Anni-Frid Lyngstad (brunette) attempted solo careers. Faltskog did manage an American top twenty success with Can't Shake Loose in 1983 but after her short lived marriage to Swedish Surgeon Tomas Sonnenfeld in 1990 she drifted out of the business to concentrate on her property investments before re-emerging in 1996 with the release of an autobiography and compilation CD.

Frida married Prince Ruzzo Reuss of Denmark in 1992 and has become heavily involved in green issues, heading a Swedish organisation called Artists For The Environment. In 1997 she released Aven en Blomma – her first single for 12 years. Benny and Bjorn have continued to write,

successfully collaborating with Tim Rice to produce the stage musical Chess and have now launched their latest work – Fran Duvenala – which opened in Malmo. 1992 saw an ABBA revival prompted by English group Erasure, leading to the release of a greatest hits album which went on to sell more than three million copies.

ABC's Martin Fry (left) and Fiona Russell (right)

ABC

Martin Fry and Mark White met in 1977 while at Sheffield University and enjoyed great success with When Smokey Sings and their album Lexicon of Love. Fry sadly developed Hodgkinsons disease in 1985 which greatly restricted the group's activity for some time. Since 1991 Fry has been recording with Parlaphone records and made a comeback in 1997 with the release of their first album for five years and a nation-wide tour. Fiona Russell, in the original line up, hit the headlines in the same year when she issued a writ against TV presenter Clive James claiming that a sexually charged character in one of his books was based on her.

ABBOT, Russ

Five times winner of the TV Times Funniest Man on Television award, Abbot earns a mention here due to his top ten single Atmosphere in 1984.

He started his career as a drummer and formed the Black Abbots before breaking through as a comedian. Latterly his wings have spread further to incorporate acting, starring as Ted Fenwick in three series of September Song.

AC/DC

AC/DC

Although formed in Australia, brothers Angus and Malcolm Young originated from Scotland, so it was appropriate that Britain became the launching pad for world-wide success. Fronted by Angus dressed in schoolboy attire, they gained a reputation for being the archetypal bad boy heavy metal band but also managed to become one of the most successful groups of their kind during the 1970s and 1980s. The hard living took its toll when lead singer Bon Scott drank himself to death in 1980. His replacement Brian Johnson previously experienced chart success as lead vocalist with Geordie whose single All Because of You peaked at No. 6 in 1973. The band's abrasive style has continued to be popular throughout the 1990s, playing to full houses around the world and selling records by the million.

ACE, Johnny

A little known American ballard singer whose death in 1954 was attributed to a gunshot wound sustained whilst playing Russian Roulette.

ACE

Pub rock band who had a 1974 top ten with How Long. Following the break up three years later lead singer Paul Carrack briefly joined Squeeze, then became a member of Mike & The Mechanics before pursuing a solo career. His 1996 album included a re-make of How Long which when released as a single again crept into the top 40.

ADAM & THE ANTS

Having previously been involved in the punk explosion of 1977, it was not until the early 1980s that Adam & The Ants achieved any major success. From then on however, the swashbuckling image of Adam Ant led the way to number ones with Stand and Deliver, Prince Charming and Goody Two Shoes. After making an appearance at Live Aid, Ant (born Stuart Goddard) moved over to the United States in 1985 to break into the acting profession. He has since appeared in numerous television shows including Northern Exposure and The Equaliser. More recently he returned home to tread the boards at London's Drill Hall in Jo Ortons Funeral Games. Ant lovers will enjoy a planned boxed set of CDs being released to celebrate an unbelievable twenty years of Ant Music.

A-HA

In 1993 the Norwegian trio were still their country's bestselling act. Morten Harket left to go solo, however his most recent release was criticised by the Norwegian press who suggested that he returned to singing in English! Despite this he still won Musician Of The Year and Best Male Artist in Norway for 1996. Pal is now a member of a group called Savoy. Mags and Morten have guested on their former bass player's solo album and Mags created a woodcut shown on the cover. Mags, who is spending more time on his artistic pursuits, also designed a range of bottles launched by a Norwegian Hotel Group and his latest batch of paintings were prepared for an exhibition in Hong Kong.
The Sun Always Shines On TV (1985).

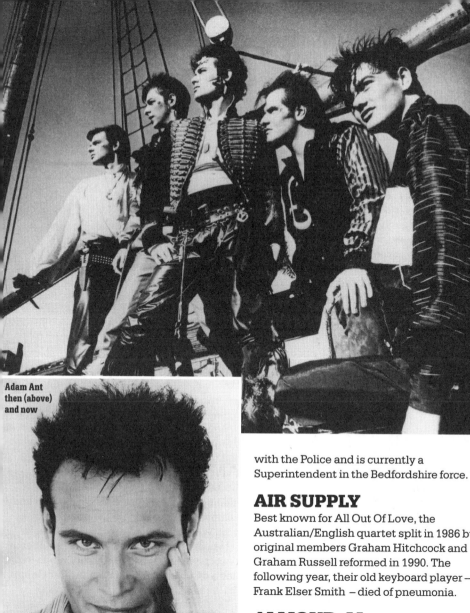

Adam Ant then (above) and now

AFTER THE FIRE

Christian band formed in the 1980s by former Yes guitarist Pete Banks. Although they struggled to make any impression on the charts, their 1983 single Der Kommissar did gain much radio airplay. These days Banks is managing director of a computer company, while the band's drummer – Ivor Twiddell – has made an outstanding success of a career

with the Police and is currently a Superintendent in the Bedfordshire force.

AIR SUPPLY

Best known for All Out Of Love, the Australian/English quartet split in 1986 but original members Graham Hitchcock and Graham Russell reformed in 1990. The following year, their old keyboard player – Frank Elser Smith – died of pneumonia.

ALMOND, Marc

Camp vocalist who hit the top spot both as a member of Soft Cell (Tainted Love in 1981) and with Gene Pitney (Something's Gotten Hold Of My Heart in 1989). Still playing solo, but returned from a period of relative quiet to form an unlikely partnership with the 1960s trouser splitter, PJ Proby.
Tainted Love (1981).

ALBERT, Morris

Lost a well publicised case accusing him of plagarising Louise Gaste's Pour Toi which he paraded as Feelings. The case cost him dear and he returned to his Brazilian homeland where he still performs.

ALBERTO Y LOST TRIOS PARANOIAS

Maniacal Jimmy Hibbert went on to write and provide voices for the television cartoon Count Duckula. Tony Bowers, the group's bass guitarist, re-emerged as a member of Simply Red. Had a Heads Down No Nonsense Mindless Boogie in 1978.

ALLISONS, The

Britain's entrants to the 1961 Eurovision Song Contest who subsequently reappeared over the years as writers, producers and artists. Despite publicity to the contrary, The Allisons were not real brothers. John Alford, now 56, lives in Lincoln now takes pride in his naturism and claims being naked feels sexy. Are You Sure earned them a gold disc and the runners up slot in the 1961 Eurovision Song Contest.

Herb Alpert

ALPERT Herb

An extraordinary musician, Alpert's trumpet playing earned him five No. 1 hits, seven Grammy awards, 15 gold albums and 14 platinum albums. His Tijuana Brass propelled Latino music into the pop music limelight and his partner, Jerry Moss, made A&M Records into the largest independent record company in the world. In the last two decades he has emerged as a talented painter with international exhibitions as well as producing stage plays on Broadway. His most serious contribution is the Herb Alpert Foundation which has six educational and arts environment programmes dedicated to the training of young people.

Clare Grogan of Altered Images

ALTERED IMAGES

Happy Birthday and I Could Be Happy were both massive hits in 1981 for the lively group led by Scottish singer Clare Grogan. She also appeared in the film Gregory's Girl and resumed her acting career (Eastenders) when the group fizzled out in 1983.

AMEN CORNER

Guitarist Andy Fairweather-Low is now a member of Eric Clapton's backing band and achieved solo success in the mid-Seventies with Wide Eyed and Legless. Blue Weaver (keyboards) went on to become a member of the Strawbs and with drummer Dennis Byron had a disco revival spell with the Bee Gees. *(If Paradise Is) Half As Nice (1969).*

AMERICA

Three man band whose brief British popularity evolved from their 1972 single A Horse With No Name. Despite a distinct lack of UK success since, original members Dewey Bunnell and Gerry Beckley have established a loyal following at home in the States.

ANDERSON, Laurie

In 1992 this former history teacher published a book called Stories From The Nerve Bible. Most recently released a live album recorded at London's Saddlers Wells called The Ugly One With Jewels . *O Superman (1987).*

ANDERSON, Lynn

Country girl Anderson struck gold with Rose Garden in 1971 but failed to capitalise on this, her only British chart entry. After spending several years based in Nashville, she returned to her native California and has recorded infrequently since, although a Greatest Hits album was released in 1992 with moderate success.

ANIMALS

While the nation was still talking about the Great Train Robbery five lads from the north-east were striking pop gold with the now legendary House Of The Rising Sun. The thirty-plus years since have seen Ronnie Biggs & Co enjoy mixed fortunes while the song has become a rock classic being copied by at least forty artists. Alan Price (keyboards) left to go solo in 1965 and the rest of the band split up the following year.

Although still a popular act, chart success has eluded him since enjoying a string of hits with Georgie Fame then solo with The Jarrow Song. Bass guitarist Chas Chandler went on to manage some of the top names including Jimi Hendrix who he discovered playing in a New York cafe and Seventies rockers Slade. He died of a heart attack in July 1996 at the age of 57.

Eric Burdon meanwhile disappeared from the music scene for two years before re-emerging with the band War. He then went into semi-retirement in France and later moved to the west coast America. In 1990 he toured with Robby Krieger, formerly of the Doors, and ironically also had a cameo role in Oliver Stone's film The Doors having studied acting at the Actor's Studio in Los Angeles. His latest creation is the Eric Burdon Band.

Hilton Valentine attempted a solo career but now fronts his own version of Animals II. *House of the Rising Sun (1964).*

Paul Anka then (above) and now

ANKA, Paul

One of the few Fifties teen idols who managed to maintain star status throughout the following four decades. Early success was built upon the ten million seller Diana then his repuation built as a songwriter with a stream of hit records performed by other artists including Frank Sinatra with My Way and Donny Osmonds revival of Lonely Boy and Puppy Love. Now a big draw in Las Vegas, Anka re-appeared in the charts himself in 1974 with You're Having My Baby and in 1992 with Freedom For The World with Ofra Haza.

APPLEBY, Kim

See MEL& KIM.

APPLEJACKS

Sixties pop group from Solihull who are best known for three hits in 1964 including Tell Me When and the novelty of a female bass player, Megan Davies. Don Gould set up a lawn mower business.

Former Animal Alan Price

ARCHIES

Created for a television series in similar vein to the Monkees, although The Archies happened to be cartoon characters and the human group only ever performed live on one occasion. The 1969 song Sugar Sugar firmly established both the show and the recording act, and at one time there was even an Archies restaurant in Illinois.

Songwriter Jeff Barry left in 1971 to work for Paramount Pictures, while Ron Dante achieved top ten hits in Britain with Tracy and When Julie Comes Around under the name of The Cufflinks. He then went on to produce albums for Barry Manilow before becoming a prominent theatre producer on Broadway.

Sugar Sugar (1969).

Rod Argent's shop in Tin Pan Alley

ARGENT

Long haired and musically gifted, Argent were perfect for the early Seventies. Hold Your Head Up and God Gave Rock n Roll To You (also a hit for Kiss in the 1990s) provided chart recognition before vocalist Russ Ballard left in 1974 to go solo. The band finally broke up in 1976 with bass guitarist Jim Rodford joining The Kinks.

Rod Argent opened a keyboard shop in Worcester and became a producer for acts including Tanita Tikaram and also played as a session musician. Nowadays he owns a sheet music shop in Tin Pan Alley – London's Denmark Street – and is also responsible for writing a number of film and TV themes.

Russ Ballard has established himself as a successful songwriter with So you Win Again by Hot Chocolate among his many credits and Since Youv'e Been Gone being ample evidence of his ability.

John Verity is now producer to heavy metal band Saxon.

Hold Your Head Up (insert date).

ARMSTRONG, Louis

Satchmo is a jazz and blues legend, best remembered for What A Wonderful World and We Have All The Time In The World as well as his brilliant trumpet playing. Died of heart and kidney failure in New York in 1971.

What a Wonderful World (1968).

ARNOLD PP

The First Cut Is The Deepest (later covered by Rod Stewart) and Angel of the Morning established Arnold's singing credentials before she decided to combine her vocal talents with acting. She has since appeared in Jesus Christ Superstar and Starlight Express. Although still a popular session singer, her only chart entry since was in 1988 when she sung with The Beatmasters on Burn It Up.

ART OF NOISE

Anne Dudley has since excelled as a producer of film and television themes including Phil Collins' Buster and Neil Jordan's The Crying Game. Television credits include the detective series Anna Lee and Jeeves & Wooster. The band had previously combined in turn with Duanne Eddy, Max Headroom and Tom Jones to score hits in the 1980s with Peter Gunn, Paranoimi and Kiss.

ASHFORD & SIMPSON

Nikolas Ashford and Valerie Simpson (whose brother Ray sings with Village People) are still performing live as well as writing and producing other artists including Whitney Houston and Diana Ross.

Solid (No. 3 in 1985).

ASHTON GARDNER & DYKE

Tony Ashton (keyboards) and Ron Dyke (drums) from the Remo Four joined forces with Kim Gardner from the Birds (which had included Ron Wood) to join the one hit wonder club on the strength of Resurrection Shuffle. Ashton later joined Medicine Head, then Family, before forming Ashton Lord with Deep Purple member Jon Lord.

Resurrection Shuffle (No. 3 in 1971).

Jailbirds

Ten who have served time (and why)

1. Leapy Lee
   Landlord slashed in a pub brawl
2. Sly Stone
   Possession of Cannabis
3. Hugh Whitaker (Housemartins)
   Assault with an axe and arson
4. Rick James
   Assault and cocaine offences
5. Tony Jackson (Searchers)
   Provoked into pub fight
6. Frankie Lyman
   Narcotics
7. John Phillips (Mamas & Papas)
   Five years for drug offences
8. Patrick Waite (Musical Youth)
   Joyriding
9. Peter Yarrow (Peter, Paul & Mary)
   Sex Offence
10. Wilson Pickett
    Alcohol-related charges

ASTLEY, Rick

A massive star in the 1980s who managed eight successive top ten entries under the guidance of producers Stock Aitken and Waterman. He now lives in a Richmond mansion thanks to the enormous wealth accumulated during his relatively brief musical career

Never Gonna Give You Up (No. 1 in 1987).

ATOMIC ROOSTER

Rock band formed by former Crazy World Of Arthur Brown member Vince Crane and drummer Carl Palmer who established a strong following on the club and college circuit in the early Seventies and charted with The Devil's Answer (No 4 in 1971). Palmer left later that year to become a third of Emerson, Lake & Palmer. The band continued with varying line ups before disbanding in 1973. Crane reformed the band in 1979 but then laid it permanently to rest. He later became a member of Dexy's Midnight Runners before committing suicide on Valentines Day 1989 having suffered from depression.

ATWELL, Winnie

Pianist who originally hailed from Trinidad but settled in London and enjoyed popularity throughout the 1950s selling in excess of 20 million records. However, after the decline of her career and the death of her husband in 1978 she emigrated to Australia where she lived as a virtual recluse until her death in 1983 from a heart attack at the age of 69.

Let's Have A Party was the biggest of her four top ten hits in 1953/4.

ARTWOODS

Sixties band formed by Ron Wood's elder brother Art, which contained future stars Keef Hartley and Jon Lord. Hartley went on to join John Mayall's Bluesbreakers and to form his own group, while Lord made his name in Deep Purple. Malcolm Pool (bass) joined Coliseum before setting up his own art studio in Hillingdon. Art himself appropriately became a graphic designer when he finally quit the music business in 1995.

AUGER, BRIAN

Joined the R & B movement from his jazz background in 1964 to form The Trinity. Original member John McLaughlin later re-surfaced in the 1970s as The Mahavishnu Orchestra.

AVALON, Frankie

Avalon's career now spans five decades starting out as a Fifties singer, becoming a Sixties actor and now in the Nineties playing trumpet in his son's band (which also features Don Everly's son Edan). Why and Venus established him as a pop star and he also had a spell in Hollywood appearing in films The Alamo and in 1978 Grease. Father of eight children and a low handicap golfer, he now lives in San Fernando Valley California but still performs in cabaret six months of the year.

AVERAGE WHITE BAND

The current version of AWB claim to be like their native Scottish Malt - maturing over time, however, their greatest successes were achieved during the 1970s when their brand of white funk produced the hit singles Pick Up The Pieces and Cut The Cake. The group faded away in the early 1980s until Alan Gorrie and Onnie McIntyre (who were both part of the original formation in 1972) regrouped in 1989. Original guitarist Hamish

The Bachelors then (above) and now

Stewart died from an accidental heroin overdose in 1974 while in Los Angeles. Molly Duncan (sax) who moved to live in Majorca, has since ormed his own band and released an album (Out Of Order) in 1992. Roger Ball (keyboards) resumed his career as an architect although he did join the new line up for one album in 1989.

BACHELORS

The success story of Irish brothers Con and Dec McLuskey began in 1957 but it was when they changed their performing name from The Harmonicords to The Bachelors. Forty years on, they are still together performing their Sixties hits. The other original singer has his own group called John Stokes' Bachelors.

BACHMAN-TURNER OVERDRIVE

Burst onto the music scene in 1974 with You Ain't Seen Nothin Yet but faded away after a change of name later to BTO . Original members Randy Bachman and Fred Turner tried again in 1984 but their only UK success was care of Messrs Smashie and Nicey (alias Harry Enfield and Paul Whitehouse) who brought the group's rock classic song to the attention of a new audience. Bachman then formed the Randy Bachman Band.

BAD COMPANY

1995 saw a version of Bad Company still touring America featuring only Mick Ralphs and Simon Kirke as remaining original members. Singer Paul Rodgers is now a successful solo artist with a new album and British tour in 1997.
Can't Get Enough (1970).

BAD MANNERS

The sight of an overweight skinhead stomping around a stage may not be everyone's idea of fun but Buster Bloodvessel, Bad Manners frontman, has managed to entertain audiences in this way for over fifteen years since their heyday in the early 1980s. Now 24 stone and still going strong he now runs an hotel in Margate for fellow tubbies called Fatty Towers and sponsors local football team Margate.

Conga player Jimmy Scott died of pneumonia following a hard American tour. Saxophonist Chris Kane took up teaching music and was Head Of Music at the Swedish School Of London. Martin Stuart sold life insurance for a spell and now acts as a band booker. Winston Bazoonis is a registered schizophrenic and was admitted to hospital in 1981. Other original members have diverse careers including graphic designer, recording studio exec and a carpenter in Eastbourne.

BADFINGER

In April 1975 singer and co-songwriter Peter Ham hung himself at his Surrey home. He and colleague Tom Evans had written Nilsson's international hit Without You but years of battling for royalties led to depression prompting him to take his own life. Tragically, Evans also took his own life in a similar manner in 1983. The matter was controversially resolved many years later with the remaining band members despite having no part in the songwriting.
Come and Get It (1970).

BAEZ, Joan

A tireless campaigner for human rights from her home in Northern California. In 1979 she founded Humanitas International and is actively involved in human rights issues as well as continuing with live performances and recording.
The Night They Drove Old Dixie Down (1971).

Buster Bloodvessel
of Bad Manners

Long John Baldry

BALDRY, Long John

Probably best known for his massive 1967 hit recording Let The Heartaches Begin, however his influence on modern music goes deeper. He is responsible for inspiring Eric Clapton to first pick up a guitar and was later credited with discovering Rod Stewart and Elton John. The 1970s saw him on perform on the club circuit before moving to Canada in 1980. Now back on the road touring Europe, 6ft 7in Baldry is also a keen opera buff, antiques collector and the voice of Captain Robotnic on Sonic The Hedgehog!

BANANARAMA

Having become Britain's most successful girl group ever, Siobhan Fahey left in 1988 to concentrate on motherhood following her marriage to Dave Stewart (Eurythmics). She later formed Shakespears Sister with American session singer Marcella Detroit (who co-wrote Lay Down Sally with Eric Clapton). While Sara Dallin and Keren Woodward carried on under the Bananarama name, Fahey returned as Shakespears Sister in 1996 after a four year gap. In the meantime Marcy had returned to the States to continue recording.

BAND

A major force in 1960s rock music, both as a backing band for Bob Dylan and as an outfit in their own right. Fed up with touring, they parted in 1978 although they did get back together again in 1984, 1986 and 1987. In 1986 Richard Manuel, who played piano and drums, hung himself in a motel room. Levon Helm and Robbie Roberston have recorded individually, the latter with substantially more success.

BANGLES

All woman rock band who finally topped the charts in 1989 with Eternal Flame after a string of hits including Manic Monday and Walking Like An Egyptian. Lead singer Suzanna Hoffs has established herself as a solo act recording for London Records since the break up of the group in 1989. Lead guitarist Vicki Peterson now lives in New Orleans and performs with the Psycho Sisters. Michael Steele (bass) lives in San Francisco, having been in a band called Eyesore, and is now solo. Debbi Peterson (drums) formed Kindred Spirit, who opened for Joan Armatrading on her 1994 tour.

BARRIE JJ

No Charge, a 1976 No. 1, earned Barrie his place in the ranks of one hit wonders. Not surprisingly, his only other notable attempt at British success, a 1980 duet with fotball manager Brian Clough with Can't Win Em All, failed to replicate his earlier success.

His record company Power Exchange went bankrupt in 1977 and he eventually returned to Canada to work in music management.

BARRY Len

American vocalist with a high pitched voice who warbled 1-2-3 up to number three in November 1965. This and his other top ten hit Like A Baby ensure that he can still earn a crust on the lucrative cabaret circuit in the States.
1-2-3 (1965).

BASS, Fontella

Soul sister from Missouri whose European success with Rescue Me and Recovery in the mid-Sixties encouraged her to move continents. She returned to St Louis in 1985, married trumpeter Lester Bowie and now performs as a jazz artist herself.

BASSEY, Shirley

Still wowing packed houses around the world at the age of 60. The dynamic songstress has been divorced twice, had three children (daughter Samantha died in 1985 having fallen from the Clifton Suspension Bridge), and now lives in relative peace in Monte Carlo.

BATT, Mike

Had four top ten hits in 1974 with Chris Spedding (Motorbiking) dressed up as Wombles.

BAY CITY ROLLERS

Rollermania was responsible for an incredible upswing in the sales of anything tartan between 1971 and 1976. Three of the original teen heart-throbs, Eric Faulkner, Stuart Wood and Alan Longmuir re-formed and still perform under the name (now wearing a more subtle version of their famous trademark), while their original singer fronts his own version under the name of Les McKeown's Legendary Rollers. The clean cut public image was slowly tarnished with a series of incidents which included their manager Tam Paton being imprisoned for indecency charges; McKeown charged with Reckless Driving after knocking down and killing a 75 year old; Faulkener and Alan Longmuir tried to commit suicide. Later members included Billy Lyall who was to die from an AIDs related illness in 1989 and Duncan Faure who back in South Africa wrote a song for Madonna Who's That Girl? album.

More recently Alan Longmuir, the drummer, suffered a heart attack and was helped back to health by brother Derek who works as a staff nurse at Edinburgh Royal Infirmary Faulkener produces solo material via his own production label called Ricky Fender Productions. Woody is also in another band in Scotland and has produced albums for an outfit called Scottish Moods. Les McKeown lives in a village near Munich with his Japanese wife and their son.

Bay City Rollers

The Beach Boys then and now (right)

BEACH BOYS

The mere mention of the Beach Boys conjures up images of Californian sun, sand and surf. Remarkably four of the five original members are still together, the fifth, Dennis Wilson died in 1983 having drowned in a lake. In 1997 Carl Wilson was diagnosed as having the early stages of cancer but after intensive chemotherapy and radiation treatment he was passed fit to join his colleagues on tour. Brian Wilson is also working as a producer working with his daughters Carnie and Wendy among others. Mike Love is in the final stages of negotiation for his Club Kokomo to open in Las Vegas.

Beastie Boys

BEASTIE BOYS

Hip hop rap trio who in 1987 advocated that (You Gotta) Fight For Your Right To Party and followed their own advice a little too literally in 1994 when guitarist Adam Horowitz was sentenced to two years probation on a charge of assault. In contrast, Adam Yauch (bass) has become deeply involved with the fight to preserve Tibetan culture and as a result the band have performed in concert with Tibetan Garden Jangtse Monks! The third member of the trio, Mike D is now involved in the rag trade, owning a stake in the successful X Large range of clothing based in New York.

BEATLES

Stuart Sutcliffe, credited with giving the band their name, became a painter in Hamburg but died in 1962 – ironically the Beatles arrived the next day to start their third German tour. Examples of his paintings can now be found in London's Hard Rock Cafe. Original drummer Pete Best has emerged from the shadows after many years working in a Liverpool jobcentre to tour with his own band.

George Harrison became interested in Formula One racing and invested in a film company called Hand-Made Films (sold in 1984 for $8.5million) who were responsible for Monty Python's Life of Brian and The Long Good Friday. In 1988 he became a member of The Travelling Wilburys which also includes Roy Orbison, Tom Petty, Dylan and Jeff Lynne.

Ringo Starr bought a £2million penthouse off London's King's Road to add to the home he shares with ex-Bond girl Barbara Bach in the South Of France.

John Lennon was shot dead by a

Dakota Building (top). Mosaic in Central Park (above)

BELL, Archie & The Drells

After being part of the Seventies Philly sound explosion Archie Bell left his Drells behind in 1981 to start a solo career and has continued to perform in cabaret ever since.

Cliff Bennett

BENNETT, Cliff & Rebel Rousers

Bennett, having been in the forefront of the R&B boom of the late 1960s, re-emerged after a long gap by forming a group called Shanghai. This was to be a brief revival and he decided to retire from music, taking a job in advertising and later running his own export business. Now back on road and still employing his original sax players Sid Phillips and Tony Hall, his band had always been a breeding ground for talent – bass guitarist Frankie Allen went onto front The Searchers. Drummer Mickey Burt had returned to his previous profession as a plumber before receiving a call to join the band's former guitarist Chas Hodges in a group he had put together with Dave Peacock – Chas Hodges had become half of Chas & Dave!
Got To Get You Into My Life (1966).

BENNETT, Tony

The old crooner who sang Left My Heart In San Francisco is now in his seventies and lives in New York overlooking Central Park. Still able to command massive fees and great ovations around the world, he has also established himself as an artist – his paintings can command as much as $50,000 each. In 1996 his For The Ladies album won him a Grammy.
Stranger in Paradise (1955).

deranged fan ouside his apartment block in New York.

Paul McCartney is now Sir Paul and his most recent music has taken a classical turn.

BECK, Jeff

See YARDBIRDS.

BELAFONTE, Harry

New York born Belafonte became an internationally famous singer almost by accident. After two years in the US Navy he tried his hand as an actor but gave up showbusiness completely, feeling totally disillusioned. It was only after buying a small restaurant with friends in Greenwich Village that his interest was rekindled. Harry would often be asked to sing whilst someone else played the guitar. Three top ten hits followed in the early 1950s and he also achieved success as a film and stage actor. The Banana Boat Song and Mary's Boy Child have continued to earn royalties to this day, being covered by artists all over the world. A leading figure in the Civil Rights Movement, he now lives in a New York apartment and owns a farm in upstate New York.

Chuck Berry

BENTON, Brook

One of the most successful black artists of the Sixties, Benton remained on the cabaret circuit until his death in 1988 at the age of 56 having suffered from spinal meningitis.

BERRY, Chuck

Commonly called the Father of Rock n Roll, Berry's off stage antics and on stage novelties (his famous Duck Walk for example) have often overshadowed his brilliant guitar playing. While a rising star in the Sixties he was found guilty of assaulting a fourteen year old girl despite protesting his innocence. Sadly the 1990s started in similar vein, when he was accused of indecent behaviour at his Berry Park home. The park had been built on 30 acres of land purchased in 1957 and today houses an impressive leisure complex which includes a massive guitar shaped pool. Although now in his seventies, Berry has lost none of his appeal and was still touring the world in 1997 with dates booked as far afield as Moscow and Hungary.

Dave Berry

BERRY, Dave

Originally scored a string of top 30 hits in the 1960s backed by The Cruisers, a backing band who have continued to provide a starting point for a number of first rate musicians, including future members of Led Zeppelin, Argent and 10cc.

Court Battles

Ten who have said "Yes, m'lud"

1. Jam
   Acrimonious split and share out of profits
2. Kenney Jones
   Fight for lost royalties
3. George Michael
   Finally won his release from record company
4. Ronettes
   Ten year battle between Ronnie & Phil Spector
5. Leo Sayer
   Won royalties tussle with former manager Adam Faith
6. Phil Spector
   Regained rights to To Know Him Is To Love Him and £300,000 in back royalties
7. Ken Dodd
   Famous run in with Inland Revenue
8. Boy George
   Autobiography upset a few former friends
9. Frankie Lymans Teenagers
   Won backdated royalties for Why Do Fools Fall In Love
10. Cindy Birdsong (Supremes)
    Lost $8million lawsuit against former colleagues

BERRY, Mike

Don't You Think Its Time spent twelve weeks in the charts in 1963, peaking at No. 6. However, it was to be a further seventeen years before Mike Berry's name appeared in the top ten again with The Sunshine Of Your Smile. In the meantime he had become a familiar face on television as an actor appearing in shows such as Worzel Gummidge.

BERRY, Nick

Starring as Nick Rowan in the series Heartbeat has established Berry as Britain's highest paid TV actor earning a reported £35,000 per episode. However it was his popularity as a member of the Wickes household in Eastenders that helped him achieve a No. 1 with Every Loser Wins.

BIG BOPPER

The Big Bopper became a household name on the strength of one song. It has been continually played since first being released over 35 years ago. The singer died in the same plane crash as Buddy Holly and Richie Valens in February 1959. A year after his death his composition Running Bear was an international hit for Johnny Preston.

Chantilly Lace
(1958).

BILK, Acker

Claims his success with the clarinet is because he had his two front teeth knocked out while at school. Stranger On The Shore was a No. 1 on both sides of the Atlantic in 1961 and was placed No. 3 in an all time top 100 chart. He now records with his Paramount Jazz Band, string orchestras and synthesisers and has homes in Potters Bar and Pensfold – the village where he was born – and has built himself a bungalow.

Big Country

BIG COUNTRY

Scottish band led by Stuart Adamson who had previously been co-founder member of seminal new wavers the Skids who had tasted success with Into The Valley and Working For The Yankee Dollar. 1983 saw Big Country break massively world-wide and a string of hits followed. Although the band has continued with various line-ups, they have not managed to replicate their earlier successes. Now back in the fold after several years in Florida, Adamson is again providing his unique vocal talents (when he is not hammering around the beautiful Scottish Countryside on his motorbike).
Fields Of Fire (1983).

BIGGUN, Ivor

Comedian Doc Cox brewed up the mischievously titled Winkers Song in 1978 long before becoming better known as one of Esther Rantzen's sidekicks on the BBC programme Thats Life.

BIRKIN, Jane & Serge Gainsbourg

French singer/songwriter Serge Gainsbourg secured the prize for the most overtly sexual number one in 1969 with J'taime. It was originally intended for Brigitte Bardot but she didnt like the idea of pretending to make love on record, so he recorded it with his English actress wife Jane Birkin. Gainsbourg died in March 1991 while Birkin has continued to make films – her latest offering being On Connait La Chanson (translates appropriately as You Know the Song!). Their daughter Charlotte, now 26, has also become an actress.

BLACK LACE

No party or discotheque seems to be complete without at least one rendition of Black Lace's Superman, Agadoo, or Do The Conga. Although supremely irritating, they never fail to raise people from their seats.

Even the band themselves, who now perform as a duo, freely admit that they were voted Wally Act Of The Year by all the music press and declare themselves a legend in their own lunchbox (no doubt while also counting their continuing royalties!). Original singer Alan Barton died in Road accident while on tour in Germany.

BLACK SABBATH

Formed in Birmingham almost three decades ago Sabbath were one of the earliest pioneers of heavy metal and have been in the forefront ever since. Geezer Butler is now operating G/Z/R (Geezer Butler Band) and Tony Iommi has a solo album due out in 1997, with help from former colleague Glenn Hughes. Various line-ups have straddled the years but in 1997 Iommi, Butler and Osbourne reunited for Ozzys Ozzfest – Bill Ward was apparently not invited and has therefore concentrated on his own projects which include the Mungus Shine Entertainment Company.

Tony Blackburn

BLACKBURN, Tony

Started out as a singer in Bournemouth with Al Stewart as a member of his backing band The Sabres. However, he had to wait until he was established as a well known disc-jockey before scraping into the Top 50 with So Much Love and It's Only Love in the late Sixties. Having been the first presenter to be heard on Radio One, he can now be heard in the same breakfast slot, but these days a little further down the medium wave at Capital Gold.

BLACKFOOT SUE

Recently re-formed to become part of the Seventies revival. Headed by the original songwriters and vocalists Tom Farmer and his twin brother David, they are now joined by two former members of Brian Connolly's Sweet. This has resulted in a live show featuring both Blackfoot Sue's top ten hits Standing In The Road and Sing Don't Speak together with old Sweet classics like Blockbuster and Ballroom Blitz.
Standing In The Road (1972).

BLONDIE

For three years Debbie Harry and Blondie could do no wrong. Between Denis in 1978 and Rapture in 1981, they notched up ten top ten smashes including five No. ones. Harry has continued to record but with limited success and has made a number of live appearances as a jazz/blues singer. There has even been some talk of a Blondie reunion. In between records she has also turned to acting, her latest role sees her as an ageing Hollywood madam in a TV movie, Confessions. In the mid-Eighties Harry and Blondie guitarist Chris Stein withdrew from the music scene due to Stein suffering from genetic disease pemphigus. Jimmi Destri is now producer of young talent and a session musician. Nigel Harrison is currently working as a talent scout for a record company.

BLOOM, Bobby

American singer best known for Montego Bay which made three chart entries in 1970/1 peaking at No. 3. He Committed suicide in 1974.

BLUE, Barry

Born Barry Green, this songwriter penned Lynsey de Paul's Seventies hit Sugar Me then achieved personal success in the Seventies with hits including Dancing On a Saturday Night. He is now a writer and producer working with Brotherhood Of Man, Bananarama, and Diana Ross.

BLUE MINK

Were a group of respected session musicians who combined behind Madeline Bell's powerful vocals to achieve three top ten triumphs including Meltin Pot'. They disbanded in 1975 with Herbie Flowers

(bass) going on to join Sky. Bell became a solo singer and a had a spell as a disc jockey with Radio One. Ann Odell now combines a role as a housewife with studio sessions. Ray Cooper continues to be one of the most respected session drummers and a regular in Elton John's backing band. Roger Cook and Roger Greenaway continued with their successful songwriting partnership which had started in the Sixties when they were know as David and Jonathan.

Debbie Harry of Blondie in 1978 (left) and 1993

BLUE ZOO

Shortlived stardom was centred on their 1982 hit Cry Baby Cry. Andy Overall now has a business selling wild mushrooms to London restaurants. His former colleagues are now variously employed in property, plumbing and one still in music as part of Neneh Cherry's backing band.

BLUNSTONE, Colin
see The ZOMBIES

BOND, Graham

Prominent character in the Sixties R & B boom who formed a formidable trio with Ginger Baker and Jack Bruce before they linked up with Eric Clapton to become Cream.

Bond became increasingly dependent on drugs which eventually contributed to his untimely death in 1974. Died under the wheels of a London Underground train at the age of 37.

Animated

Ten with cartoon connections

1. **Long John Baldry**
   Captain Robotic in Sonic The Hedgehog
2. **Sheena Easton**
   Sacha in All Dogs Go To Heaven
3. **Jimmy Hibbert (Alberto Y Los Trios Paranoias)**
   Voices in Count Duckula
4. **Randy Newman.**
   James & The Giant Peach music
5. **John Du Prez (Modern Romance)**
   Music for Teenage Mutant Hero Turtles
6. **Toyah Wilcox**
   Voice to Brum
7. **Ringo Starr** – voice
   Junior Campbell (Marmalade) – music
   Thomas The Tank Engine
8. **Randy Edelman**
   Care Bears Theme
9. **Keith Emerson**
   Iron Man Cartoon Theme
10. **M.C. Hammer**
    Hammer cartoon

BONEY M

Created by German producer Frank Farian (later also responsible for Milli Vanilli), who employed singers from Jamaica, Antilles and Monserrat to become one of the weirdest acts of the Seventies. In 1992 the band re-entered the English top ten after an absence of over 10 years with a megamix version of their previous hits. They had split up in 1986 but re-formed in 1991 with Liz Mitchell being the only original member. She had earlier married American actor Johnny Pemberton, only to discover that he was already married and never divorced! The male centrepiece, Bobby Farrell, was last heard of living off benefits in a council house near Amsterdam.
Rivers Of Babylon (1978).

BONZO DOG DOO-DAH BAND

Formed in 1966 by a group of eccentric art students the Bonzos scored a top five hit two years later with Urban Spaceman, produced by Paul McCartney.

The band broke up in 1970 and Roger Ruskin Spear went solo with his mad Kinetic Wardrobe. Legs Larry Smith went into session work with Elton John and Eric Clapton. Rodney Slater left the music business to work for local government. Martin Stafford and Vernon-Dudley Bohay-Nowell joined Bob Kerr's Whoppee Band. Neil Innes worked extensively with Monty Python, collaborated with Eric Idle to create The Rutles (mock-Beatles, I Must Be In Love made top 40 in 1978) and is now regularly on television including a role in kids show Wizadora. Viv Stansall appeared on Mike Oldfields Tubular Bells and wrote the film Rawlinson's End which starred Trevor Howard. He died in a fire at his London flat in 1995.

BOOKER T & The MGs

Stax session musicians led by Booker T James and Steve Cropper (who wrote In The Midnight Hour and Sitting on the Dock of The Bay). After Sixties hits Time is Tight and Green Onions they disbanded in 1972.

Cropper returned to session work with Jeff Beck, Rod Stewart and Ringo Starr and became chief recording engineer with Stax Records. Al Jackson (drums) was murdered at his home in Memphis in 1975. James (lead singer) married the sister of Rita Coolidge and embarked on a solo career. As a producer, he worked on Willie Nelson's bestseller Stardust and reformed the band in 1990 for cabaret shows. Cropper and Donald Dunn (bass guitarist) both became part of the backing band for The Blues Brothers.
Time is Tight (1969).

BOOMTOWN RATS

Six man formation from Ireland where they played a mix of reggae and R & B in local bars before moving to London to join the punk boom. Faded away post-Geldof and Live Aid having topped the charts with Rat Trap and I Don't Like Mondays. Bob Geldof's work with The Band Aid charity not only raised considerable sums, but resulted in a knighthood. Having endured a turbulent marriage to Paula Yates, he enjoyed great success with Channel 4's The Big Breakfast – produced by his own television company.

Boney M then and now (below)

BOONE, Pat

A descendant of American pioneer Daniel Boone, he consistently had at least one single in the US charts during the late-Fifties. He turned to religion and toured as The Pat Boone family show from which his daughter Debby became massive country star who had a US No. 1 with You Light Up My Life. Later Pat and Debby appeared in Vegas together for many years. Having written many bestselling books on religion he recently had his weekly gospel show cancelled by the Christian TV network because he dressed up in leather to record an album of heavy metal covers!

BOWIE, David

The chameleon of pop whose many guises have kept him at the very top of his profession since breaking into the charts in 1969 with Space Oddity. As well as unbroken musical success he has ventured into films and stage performances as The Elephant Man on Broadway. In 1997 life turned full circle for the former London Art College student when his rejuvenated interest in the arts culminated in his involvement with various projects including an exhibition of his own work.

BOY GEORGE

See CULTURE CLUB.

BRAMBELL Wilfred & CORBETT Harry H

Better known as Steptoe & Son this unlikely duo enjoyed a novelty success in 1963 with At The Palace (Parts 1 & 2). Brambell, who was relatively unknown until he was in his fifties when he finally won the part of spindly unshaven Alfred Steptoe, died of cancer in 1985. Harry H died several years later.

BREAD

American vocal group who failed to crack the UK charts themselves before breaking up in 1973 – three versions of their songs achieved the feat when recorded by other artists: a reggae version of Everything I Own for Ken Boothe (1974); If by Telly Savalas the following year and in 1987 Everything I Own by Boy George completed the remarkable hat-trick.

Bread got back together again in 1977 but only lasted a few months before they split. Lead singer Gates retired to an 800 acre ranch in California became a solo singer. Larry Knetchell, the band's bass player and guitarist moved to Nashville, recording his own albums and appearing in Elvis Costello's band. Drummer Mike Botts writes jingles and works on children's albums.
Everything I Own (1972).

Bros then (left) and Luke Goss now

Brotherhood of Man

BRESSLAW, Bernard

Giant comedy actor who starred as Popeye in the Army Game and was a regular member of the Carry On team. Died from a heart attack in 1993.

Mad Passionate Love (1958).

BRONSKI BEAT

See JIMMY SOMERVILLE.

BROS

Comprised of Matt Goss and his brother Luke, who after an acrimonious split with Bass guitarist Craig Logan could not maintain their enormous popularity for long. A two year purple patch in the late-Eighties had young girls screaming for the two blond brothers and provided a succession of hits, but apparently not the wealth that you would have expected. High living meant that they made millions but came away with nothing. Luke set up own unsuccessful band, then went into theatre playing small parts in small theatres. He has starred in Grease on the West End stage following a coach tour around the country with the show What a Feeling with fellow Eighties stars Sonia and Sinitta. Matt is still singing. Logan was made International Marketing Manager at EMI Records in September 1995 and has been the partner of former Mel & Kim singer Kim Appleby for many years.

BROTHERHOOD OF MAN

Original lead singer Tony Burrows had hits with Ivy League, Flowerpot Men and Edison Lighthouse before fronting Brotherhood of Man. Their 1986 Eurovision Song Contest winning entry Save All Your Kisses For Me topped the hit parade in 36 countries. These days, all four original members are still together keeping the name of Brotherhood Of Man alive on the cabaret circuit.

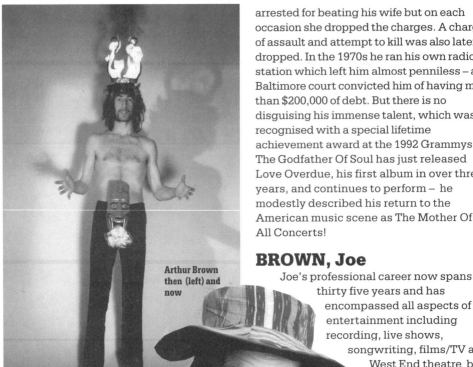

Arthur Brown then (left) and now

arrested for beating his wife but on each occasion she dropped the charges. A charge of assault and attempt to kill was also later dropped. In the 1970s he ran his own radio station which left him almost penniless – a Baltimore court convicted him of having more than $200,000 of debt. But there is no disguising his immense talent, which was recognised with a special lifetime achievement award at the 1992 Grammys. The Godfather Of Soul has just released Love Overdue, his first album in over three years, and continues to perform – he modestly described his return to the American music scene as The Mother Of All Concerts!

BROWN, Joe

Joe's professional career now spans thirty five years and has encompassed all aspects of entertainment including recording, live shows, songwriting, films/TV and West End theatre both as principal actor and director. He has presented several television series, three series of the Joe Brown show and has established himself as a popular DJ on Radio 2. In addition to all this he has also managed to write his first book (Brown Sauce). Daughter Sam, hit the top ten with Stop in 1989 – 26 years after her fathers last appearance in the same exalted position.

BROWN, Arthur

Appeared in the film version of Tommy in the Seventies and The God Of Hellfire has now returned to England after twenty years of living in Austin, Texas, where he had set up a decorating and carpentry business with Frank Zappa's former drummer Jimmy Carl Black. He has a new Crazy World band, a new album in the making, an autobiography about to be published and a guest role in the Rock Proms along side Roger Daltrey.
Set his hat alight in 1968.

BROWN, James

James Brown has risen from being a juvenile delinquent to a soul music godfather who at one time broke the box-office record in every single black music venue in America. Despite this, involvement with drugs and run-ins with the law seemed to become the norm from thereon. Three times he has been

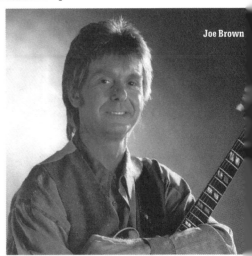

Joe Brown

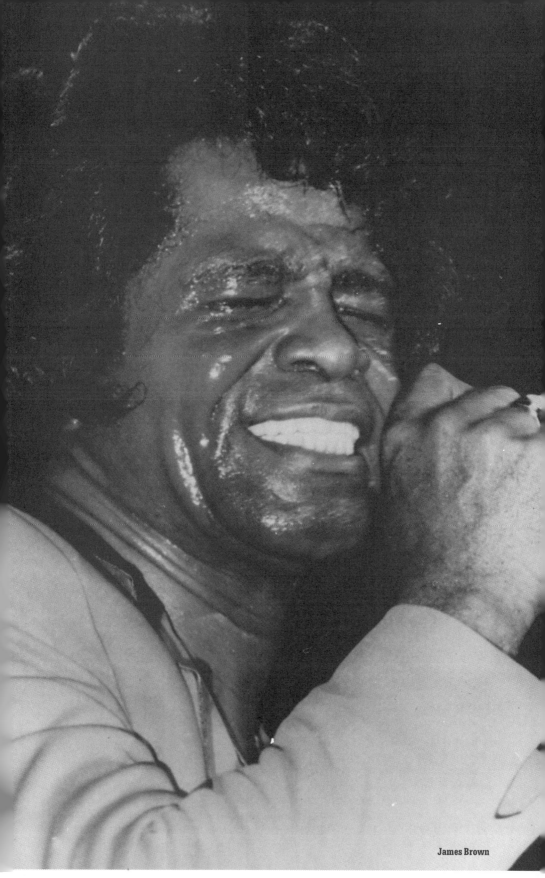

James Brown

Bucks Fizz

BROWNE, Jackson

American folk singer who scored a minor success in 1994 with Everywhere I Go – sixteen years after Stay had first brought him British chart success. His 1993 album I'm Alive chronicled his break up from actress Daryl Hannah and he has since been performing in a number of charity concerts for causes ranging from anti-apartheid to AIDS. He returned to Britain in 1997 to headline the Cambridge folk festival.

BUCKLEY, Jeff

American songwriting son of Tim Buckley who by the time of his death in 1997 had built up a devoted following and an ability to mesmerise his live audiences. He died in bizarre and tragic circumstances by drowning in the River Mississippi having last been seen floating on his back with guitar in hand. His father Tim died in 1975 from a heroin overdose.

BUCKS FIZZ

The Eurovision Song Contest plays a central role in the history of pop quartet Bucks Fizz. In addition to their 1981 wining entry Making Your Mind Up, Cheryl Baker had been part of Co-Co (represented the UK in 1978), and Jay Aston's brother Lance was in Prima Donna (winners in 1980). Since 1989 various line-ups have kept the name alive. The current quartet includes one original member, former self-employed builder Bobby Gee, who is joined by former Guys & Dolls and Dollar member David Van Day. Karen Logan also joined having been in Dollar but returned returned home to the Highlands in 1996 to spend more time with her family. Jay Aston who had left the group following an affair with the group's songwriter Andy Hill now has her own fan club and has recorded an as yet unreleased album Lamb Or Lizard. Her replacement, Shelley Preston, became a backing singer for Wet Wet Wet and Jason

B

Donovan among others. Cheryl Baker has married former Bucks Fizz guitarist Steve Stroud and currently presents no less than three weekly television programmes, including Record Breakers. As well as running in the London Marathon, she has scored a major success in a different chart – Cheryl Bakers Low Calorie Cook Book reached number four in the bestsellers list.

BUGGLES
See YES.

BURNETTE, Johnny
Born in Memphis, Tennessee, Burnette had attended the same school as Elvis Presley before becoming a teen idol on the strength of his hit You're Sixteen. He died in a boating accident on Clear Lake, California in 1964 aged only 30. His memory has been kept alive by Ringo Starr's successful cover of You're Sixteen in 1974, and the success of Burnette's son Rocky, who is now a popular recording artist in his own right.

BURROWS, Malandra
Now back safely snuggled up by the fire in Emmerdale Farm after a flirtation with the pop charts which resulted in Just This Side Of Love reaching number 11 in 1990.

BYRDS
While US troops started fighting in Vietnam, the Byrds, who topped the British charts with Dylan's Mr Tambourine Man, had to fight a battle of their own – upon arrival for a UK tour they were met by an English group, called the Birds, who wanted to legally prevent them from using a similar name. The guitarist with the British plaintiffs was none other than future Rolling Stone Ronnie Wood!

Since their last ever concert in 1973 three original members have died. Gram Parsons went solo but died in 1973 from a heroin overdose; founder member and drummer Michael Clarke died of liver disease in Florida in December 1993. He had left the band in 1969 to join the Flying Burrito Brothers with fellow ex-Byrd Chris Hillman.

Shortly after the Byrds broke up Clarence White was killed by a drunk driver. Gene Clark died at home on Bob Dylan's 50th birthday in 1991. Of the others, Kevin Kelly went back to music school but has not been heard of for many years. Gene Parsons became involved with the manufacturing of the Parsons/White string-bender pulley device for guitarists and performs with his wife Meridian under the name of Parsons-Green. Chris Hillman is now a solo artist and has recently started recording again. Skip Battin, the oldest living Byrd, still plays in the Byrds Celebration which contains no original members.

Roger McGuinn effectively retired from recording through the Eighties when he preferred to restrict his live performances to small venues. Dave Crosby founded Crosby, Stills, Nash, & Young as well as discovering and then producing folk icon Joni Mitchell. In the 1980s he was involved in car crashes, court cases, was incarcerated in a Texas prison and wrote his best selling autobiography. He nearly died in 1994 but after a liver transplant and help from a personal trainer claims to be fitter than ever. *Mr Tambourine Man (1965).*

Band Hoppers
Ten who have played musical chairs

1. Ray Stiles (Mud)
   Now in The Hollies
2. David Van Dey (Dollar)
   Now in Bucks Fizz
3. Ron Wood (The Faces)
   Now in the Rolling Stones
4. Frankie Allen (Cliff Bennetts Rebel Rousers)
   Now in The Searchers
5. Bob Jackson (Badfinger)
   Now in the Fortunes
6. Brian Johnson (Geordie)
   Now in AC/DC
7. Chas Hodges and Mickey Burt (Cliff Bennetts Rebel Rousers)
   Now in Chas and Dave
8. Farmer Twins (Blackfoot Sue)
   Became part of Brian Connolly's Sweet (before Brians death)
9. Scott McKenzie
   Now in Mamas & Papas
10. Dave Dee
    Performs regularly with Marmalade

C & C MUSIC FACTORY

After the 1991 hit Things That Make You Go Hmmm David Cole went on to become a producer and pianist. He died in March 1995 at the age of 32 from spinal meningitis.

C Roy

Shotgun Wedding was first recorded in 1966 and charted again in the UK in 1972. Roy C then moved behind the scenes to set up his own record label – Alaga Records.

CCS

Formed by R & B giant Alexis Korner, the band enjoyed mainstream success with Tap Turns On The Water and the long term Top Of The Pops theme Whole Lotta Love. Korner died from cancer in January 1984.

Tap Turns On The Water (1971).

CALVERT, Eddie

Trumpeter who spent five weeks at No. 1 in 1954 with O Mein Papa – the first instrumental record to sell over 3 million copies. At the end of the Sixties Calvert left for South Africa where he had been appointed Entertainment Officer between the Bantu people and the South African Government. He died from a heart attack in Johannesburg in 1978. His Zambesi and Cherry Pink And Apple Blossom White provided 1982 hits for the Pirahanas and Modern Romance.

CAMPBELL, Junior

See MARMALADE.

CANNED HEAT

Woodstock Festival and the hippy 1960s provided the backdrop to Canned Heat's rise to fame. Let's Work Together and On The Road Again, both top ten singles, brought them world-wide recognition and a version of the band are still playing under the same name but with no original members. Founder member and guitarist Al Wilson was found dead in Bob Hite's garden in California in 1970 and in April 1981 singer Hite died of a heart attack at the age of 38.

CAPTAIN BEEFHEART

Has now reverted back to his real name, Don Van Vlieta. The former rock heavyweight has become a respected artist with frequent exhibitions and his works fetching high prices.

CAPTAIN SENSIBLE

See THE DAMNED.

CAPTAIN & TENILLE

Daryl Dragon, the captain, and Toni Tennille stayed together as a married couple despite the pressures of show business. Daryl had previously been with the Beach Boys in 1967 and stayed with them for six years, playing keyboards and assisting with musical arrangements.

Do That To Me One More Time in 1980 was the duo's only real chart success, after which their recording career came to an abrupt end because of troubles at their record label. Toni went solo covering classic standards and continues to be involved with that kind of music today. Daryl still appears on keyboards for the Beach Boys. Toni and Daryl also own one of the most successful recording studios in California – Rainbow Recorders is considered to be one of the top three studios in Los Angeles.

CARMEN, Eric

Following the dissolution of The Raspberries in 1975 Carmen, the group's singer and primary songwriter, briefly found solo fame with the 1976 single All By Myself. It was to be a further ten years before his Hungry Eyes from the film Dirty Dancing returned him to the charts. He continues to perform and another decade has passed which may well mean he is due for his next hit!

All By Myself (1976).

CARNES, Kim

Now lives in a 75-acre estate in Nashville. purchased as a result of her continued success as a songwriter. Won a Grammy Award for Bette Davis Eyes (No. 10 in 1981).

CARPENTERS

On February 4th 1983 Karen was found unconscious by her mother at her parent's home in Downey. She died of heart failure as a result of her long battle with the disease Anorexia Nervosa and is now buried at the Forest Lawn Memorial Park. Her brother Richard became a producer and is currently employed by the Disney Corporation as a musical director. In 1994 The Karen and Richard Carpenter Performing Arts Centre in Carelstate University, Longbeach was

Bizarre Deaths

Died a gruesome death

1 Johnny Ace
   Russian Roulette
2 Paul Jeffreys (Cockney Rebel)
   Lockerbie Air Disaster
3 Graham Bond
   Under A Tube Train
4 Al Jackson (Booker T & MGs) and
   Peter Tosh (Wailers)
   Shot By Burglars
5 Johnny Burnette
   On A Fishing Trip
6 Sam Cooke
   Shot By Woman Following Alleged Rape
7 Michael Menson (Double Trouble)
   Soaked In Petrol and Set Alight
8 Marvin Gaye
   Shot By His Own Father
9. Viv Stanshall (Bonzo Dog Band)
   and Steve Marriott (Small Faces)
   Died In House Fires
10 Keith Relf (Yardbirds)
   Electrocuted

opened and the call for Carpenters material is still as strong today with several collections having been released to satisfy demand.

CARROTT, Jasper
A star turn in the folk clubs of Birmingham until 1975 when his Funky Moped brought national recognition. Although the flowing curly locks may have gone, his presence on our television screens has been consistently maintained most recently in the Detectives with Robert Powell. His heart and home are still in Brum where one of his best mates is ELO drummer Bev Bevan.

CASH, Johnny
The Man In Black famed for his Boy Named Sue (No. 4 in 1969) and A Thing Called Love three years later has managed to keep abreast of trend changes, largely by collaborating with contemporary artists like Bruce Springsteen and Nick Lowe. His daughter Roseanne has inherited her father's musical ability and has emerged as one

Country Music's foremost singer-songwriters.

CASSIDY, David
Cassidy always wanted to be a performer since watching his father, the actor Jack Cassidy, on stage and achieved his aim as a member of TV's Partridge Family. Although this became the springboard for his success, he later described the experience as 'a nightmare'. He drove the girls wild and topped the charts with How Can I Be Sure? and Daydreamer/The Puppy song before breaking their hearts by marrying actress Kay Lenz and retiring from showbusiness to live in Hawaii.

With two failed marriages behind him, he moved to England in 1984 and backed by George Michael The Last Kiss returned him to the UK top 10. He has since appeared on stage in Joseph And The Amazing Technicolour Dreamcoat, replaced Cliff Richard in Time, and starred with his brother Sean in Blood Brothers both on Broadway and in London's West End. Now living in California with his wife Sue Schifrin and son Beau, he wrote his memoirs called C'mon Get Happy: Fear And Loathing In The Partridge Family Bus.

CASSIDY, Shaun
Also a member of the Partridge Family, he went on to star in The Hardy Boys television show but could not break out of the teeny-bopper mould. He recorded some rock tunes in 1979 and 1980 but American radio had already forgotten him. He still continues to act, primarily in the theatre, and spent one summer appearing in General Hospital on TV. He married a former model in 1991 and is now content to continue a career in acting and producing. He was on the Broadway stage in 1993 as a co-star with David Cassidy in Blood Brothers.

CETERA, Peter
See CHICAGO.

CHAPIN, Harry
Chapin enjoyed a glittering musical career before his premature death in 1981 however it was as a film-maker that he first made his mark. In 1969 Legendary Champions, a documentary that he had made in

Plane Death

Ten who perished in plane crashes

1 Big Bopper *1959*
2 Richie Valens *1959*
3 Buddy Holly *1959*
4 Patsy Cline *1963*
5 Jim Reeves *1964*
6 Otis Redding *1967*
7 Jim Croce *1973*
8 Ronnie Van Zant & Steve Gaines
    (both Lynryd Skynryd) *1977*
9 Rick Nelson *1985*
10 John Denver *1997*

conjunction with Jim Jacobs was nominated for an Oscar. Commercial success with numerous albums and notably his singles Cats In The Cradle and WOLD followed, earning the singer/songwriter a host of awards including a Grammy for best Pop Vocal Performer in 1974 and being honoured for Outstanding Public Service at the Annual Rock Music Awards show two years later.

His most prestigious citation was bestowed posthumously six years after the fatal car accident that took his life in honour of his charity work which had raised over $5 million – he was awarded the Special Congressional Gold Medal, an honour given to only 114 US Citizens.

CHARLES, Ray

When Ill Be Good To You entered the British charts in 1990, it ended a twenty-two year absence for one of the greatest blues artists of all time. Blinded at the age of seven, Charles was born Ray Robinson but reverted to his middle name to avoid confusion with boxer Sugar Ray. Hit The Road Jack and his only UK No. 1 and I Can't Stop Loving You still provides inspiration for a new generation of budding singers.

CHARLES, Tina

In the Nineties former disco diva Tina has been in popular demand due to the Seventies revival. Her latest venture is in partnership with Shakatak and they have recently recorded a new single titled Only A Woman.

CHAS & DAVE

see CLIFF BENNETT.

CHECKER, Chubby

Former chicken packer whose name was inspired by Fats Domino – Chubby=Fats; Checker=Domino! The man who made the most of the twist married former Miss World Dutch beauty Catherine Lodder and featured in the rock movie Let The Good Times Roll. The Nineties saw him appear in Nabisco's most successful advertising campaign ever and Checker trying to introduce the Texas Twist. Accompanied by his Wildcats, he still performs almost 300 dates a year and but was described by a fellow artist as being 'as bald as a coot and wearing a wig'.
Let's Twist Again (1961, 1975, 1988).

CHEECH & CHONG

Richard Cheech Marin and Tommy Chong became cult figures in the Sixties selling millions of their drug based satirical albums. The duo finally split in 1985 and Marin concentrated on acting while Chong acted and directed. Chong's daughter Rae Dawn has since surpassed her father's acting achievements.
Basketball Jones (1973).

CHIC

Disco group formed by Nile Rogers and Bernard Edwards. In the Eighties following their run of big chart successes, Edwards worked as a successful producer for Rod Stewart and Robert Palmer but was also reported to have a drug problem. He died in April 1996 at the age of 43 while touring with the band in Japan – his former partner Rogers discovered the body.

CHICAGO

A major force in power rock circles before their 1976 smash If You Leave Me Now. The hit has since been described by founder member Robert Lamm as probably the worst thing to happen to the group. After a period of pandering to the needs of a pop audience the band has now returned to its roots and recording on their own record label. Singer Peter Cetera left in the mid-Eighties, charting himself with Glory Of Love in 1986. Original member Terry Kath died in 1978

Chicory Tip

from a self inflicted accidental gunshot wound. In 1997 a new CD and book were released to celebrate Chicago's 30th anniversary.

CHICORY TIP

Son Of My Father, one of Georgio Moroders early production successs brought Chicory Tip their biggest smash in 1972. Two lesser efforts followed during the height of the glam rock boom and after a twenty year gap they are now back touring on the circuit.
Son Of My Father (1972).

CHIFFONS

The Chiffons biggest British success was with Sweet Talkin' Guy which hit the top five six years after its first release when it had barely scraped into the top forty. In 1992 Barbara Lee Jones suffered a heart attack at the age of 48, but they still continue to perform throughout the States.

CHI-LITES

The Chi-Lites have been together for 26 years

and are responsible for classic R&B and pop songs Have You Seen Her? and Homely Girl. They are currently still recording their own brand of easy listening soul music for Ditchie Band Records based in Atlanta and still tour.

CHIPMUNKS

Created by Ross Bagdasaiaran who had previously had a hit in the Fifties under the name of David Seville with Witch Doctor. He died in January 1972 but the Chipmunks were later revived by his son Ross Jnr.

CHRISTIANS

English soulsters of Liverpudlian origin whose version of the Isley Brothers hit Harvest For The World broke into the top ten in 1988. They were involved with the chart topping charity version of Ferry Across the Mersey the following year and although they are still together as a band, they have failed to make any major commercial impact since their album Colours reached the top of the album charts in 1990.

41

Dave Clark Five

CHRISTIE

Still performing and fronted by Jeff Christie who wrote the 1970 chart-topper Yellow River. Jeff also enjoys a solo career as songwriter, recording artist and performer.

CHRISTIE, Lou

In 1969 his I'm Going to Make You Mine reached No. 2 in England and prompted the American singer's move to England. He ran the Five Arts company, became a band manager and made TV adverts. In the Nineties he has cut down on his musical commitments and is now only performing occasionally for night club audiences but has also had a variety of jobs outside music including cattle-farming and offshore oil drilling.

CHRISTIE, Tony

Yorkshire's answer to the Las Vegas style cabaret performer, Christie triumphed with I Did What I Did For Maria and Is This The Way To Amarillo in 1970-1972. Despite appearing on the studio cast album of Evita in 1978, he is now predominately found entertaining diners on the British cabaret circuit.

CITY BOY

Pub-rock band from Birmingham whose energetic 5-7-0-5, a 1978 top ten single, proved to be their chart high point. Vocalist Lol Mason subsequently formed The Maisonettes who charted in 1982 with Heartache Avenue. He has since concentrated on writing scripts for television and radio, winning the Radio Times

became a successful Estate Agent in Bournmouth. Rick Huxley (guitarist) has his own Electrical business and Lenny Davidson owns several antique shops. Dave himself produces records, wrote the West End musical Time and shrewdly purchased the rights to the 1960s television show Ready Steady Go.

CLARK, Petula

Appeared in more than twenty major films as well as being one of Britain's foremost female singers since her first hit over forty years ago. In 1977 she went into semi-retirement in Geneva and worked infrequently before establishing a new career on the stage. She starred as Maria in a spectacular revival production of the hit musical The Sound of Music in 1982 – her first-ever appearance in a stage musical – 14 years later she was again treading the boards, this time in Sunset Boulevard.

CLASH

Archetypal Punk band with a political stance who broke up in 1986 but five years later scored a posthumous No. 1 with Should I Stay Or Should I Go which had been popularised by a Levis commercial. Mick Jones moved on to form Big Audio Dynamite and Joe Strummer became increasingly involved with Amnesty International and in 1997 released Generations – A Punk Look At Human Rights. Strummer guested with Black Grape on Top of the Tops – whilst fronting the Clash he had sworn that they would never appear on the programme. He now has a recording studio in Brighton.

Annual Radio Comedy award in 1991. Roy Ward, who also sang on their big hit also provided the voice for Tight Fit's The Lion Sleeps tonight. Keyboard player Max Thomas took up teaching maths.

CLARK, Dave FIVE

The beginning of 1964 with Beatlemania at its peak, saw the emergence of one of the biggest acts in the Sixties – The Dave Clark Five. Their footstomping Glad All Over knocked Liverpool's Fab Four from the top of the charts and became the first of a string of hits. The group broke up in 1970 and in 1978 a compilation album entitled Twenty Five Thumping Great Hits put them back at the top of the British album charts. Denis Payton

CLIFF, Jimmy

Jamaican reggae singer who moved to Britain where producer Chris Blackwell signed him to Island Records. He starred in the reggae movie, The Harder They Come, which hoisted him to international stardom. It gained a cult following all over the world and Jimmy was able to spread his own kind of word about the plight of black people by performing his reggae gospel. Jimmy, now living in Somerton, St. James has spent recent years touring what he calls 'the Third World' and today looks upon himself as a musical messenger.
Beautiful People (1969).

CLINE, Patsy

Although a true Country star, Patsy Cline's emotional singing style earned her mainstream acclaim. Her biggest British chart success was in 1990 with Crazy which reached No. 14, 27 years after her death in a plane crash in March 1963.

CLOONEY, Rosemary

Rock n roll effectively ended the chart career of one of the Fifties' most popular female singers, but not before a period of top ten domination between 1952 and 1955. She has since published her autobiography detailing her time in a psychiatric ward which was made into a television film called Escape From Madness. New life was given to one of her biggest hits when Shakin Stevens topped the charts in 1981 with This Ole House more than 25 years after Clooney had achieved the same feat.

COASTERS

The group starred in the film Let The Good Times Roll and have now been around since 1957, becoming the first vocal group ever to be inducted to the Rock n roll Hall Of Fame. Original member Cornelius Gunter was shot while in his car in Las Vegas in 1990, but the rest of The Coasters are still performing on the oldies circuit and are regularly used by Joan Rivers as her opening act.
Yakety Yak (1958).

Joe Cocker

COCHRAN, Eddie

Rock n Roll legend Eddie Cochran was killed in a car crash on the A4 during his 1960 tour of England – Gene Vincent, who was in the same car, was badly injured. Twenty-eight years later, his song C'mon Everybody reached No. 14 in the UK charts having been given a new lease of life by a Levis jeans commercial.

COCKER, Joe

After an appearance at Woodstock and With A Little Help From My Friends had briefly lifted him to international stardom

Eddie Cochran

in the late Sixties, Cocker returned to Britain and drifted into semi-retirement. In 1972 he made a disastrous comeback with a world tour, taking in Australia, where he was arrested on a drugs charge and eventually deported. For the next few years his career and private life were dogged with problems – drinks, drugs, and financial troubles plagued him. He became a recluse, living off former glories on the West Coast of America.

The Sheffield lad now lives in Colorado and after a recording career spanning over 30 years released a new album in 1996 together with a video compilation containing new versions of his old hits.

COCKNEY REBEL Steve Harley &

Since disbanding in 1977 guitarist Jim Cregan (one time partner of Linda Lewis) has found alternative employment playing in Rod Stewart's backing band. Bass player Paul Jeffreys died in the Lockerbie air disaster in 1988. Harley himself moved to America before returning to the UK to star in The Phantom of the Opera. This led to a return to the UK charts with the title tune, a duet with Sarah Brightman, which reached No.7 in 1986. Now touring again with a band under the old name and still performing their Seventies standards.
(Come Up and See Me) Make Me Smile (1975).

CO-CO
See BUCKS FIZZ.

COGAN, Alma
Died of Cancer in 1966 at Londons Middlesex Hospital, having been one of the most popular female singers of her time. She scored twenty top twenty entries and became the only solo British female number one of the fifties with Dreamboat.

COLE, Nat King
Nat King Cole's greatest songs became million sellers for the smooth voiced crooner and have regularly been revived by a variety of artists since his death in February 1965. Mona Lisa, When I Fall In Love and Unforgettable have all charted in recent years, the latter being a technically created duet featuring Nat King Cole and his daughter Natalie.

COLLINS, Judy
Amazing Grace was truly amazing for this American folk singer with the song re-entering the charts seven times within two years. She has now branched out successfully in three more directions: Politically – she acted as a UNICEF spokeswoman in Vietnam and gained much publicity following a jog with President Clinton whose daughter Chelsea was named after her song Chelsea Morning! Films – she appeared in Arnold Schwarzenegger's Junior and was nominated for an Oscar for her co-production of Portrait Of A Woman. Writing – in 1995 she released a novel called Shameless published by Pocket Books in America and also an album by the same name.
Send In The Clowns (1970).

COMMODORES
The Commodores sold 60 million records for Motown before lead singer Lionel Richie left to pursue an extremely successful solo career. In 1988 their song Easy re-entered the English chart as a result of its use in a Halifax Building Society television advertisement. The group now possess their own record label – Commodores Records & Entertainment – and are still touring but with only Walter Clyde Orange and William King remain as original members.
Three Times A Lady (1978).

COMMUNARDS
A musical vehicle for Jimmy Somerville and former church organist Richard Coles to

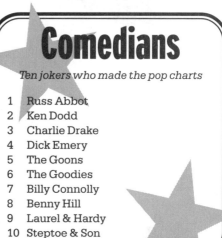

Comedians

Ten jokers who made the pop charts

1   Russ Abbot
2   Ken Dodd
3   Charlie Drake
4   Dick Emery
5   The Goons
6   The Goodies
7   Billy Connolly
8   Benny Hill
9   Laurel & Hardy
10 Steptoe & Son

scream out their distinctive and hugely popular dance tunes. At the end of 1988 Coles left to pursue a career in the media as a religious commentator.

Don't Leave Me This Way (1986).

COMO, Perry

While chocolates are advertised on television to the soothing sound of Magic Moments, the originator of the 1958 No.1, Perry Como, has been in semi-retirement for many years. However, despite being in his eighties, he still occasionally puts on his dinner suit to entertain in the clubs of Las Vegas.

CONGREGATION

Alan Parker has since directed Evita, The Commitments and Bugsy Malone as well as being Chairman of the British Film Institute.

CONLEY, Arthur

A protege of the late, great Otis Redding who had a 1967 hit with Sweet Soul

Billy
Connolly

Music. He still performs in clubs all over America and Europe .

CONNOLLY, Billy

Three jokey tunes in the Seventies helped launch the Big Yin – DIVORCE, the most successful, topping the chart in 1975. Ten years later his Super Gran TV theme song returned him to the top forty. Has since been working in America with mixed success and played a voice role in Disney's Pochahontas (as Ben) and played Billy Jones in the Muppet Treasure Island Adventure. Made a more impressive acting debut in the 1997 film Mrs Brown.

CONRAD, Jess

The man with the gleaming smile is now 60 and has been married to his Dutch model wife for 35 years. Since the Seventies he has appeared in stage musicals including Godspell and Joseph And The Amazing Technicolour Dream-Coat. Most recently played Prince Charming in Jim Davidson's spoof pantomime Sinderella.

COOK, Peter & MOORE, Dudley

Satarist supreme Cook became involved with Private Eye as both investor and contributor. His own brand of satirical humour continued to earn him a living in print and on television until his death in 1995. Dudley Moore made the film 10 in 1979 and Arthur in 1980 but his screen success has often been overshadowed by his turbulent private life, dotted with beautiful women.

Goodbye-ee (1965).

COOKE, Sam

Rod Stewart's inspiration and one of the earliest soul superstars who sold almost 20 million records including the now legendary Chain Gang and Twistin' The Night Away. His life was abruptly ended when he was shot by a woman in a Los Angeles motel who claimed that the singer had tried to rape her and accordingly a verdict of justifiable homicide was recorded. His alleged victim, Elisa Boyer, was later convicted of killing her boyfriend and prostitution.

Twistin' The Night Away (1962).

Alice
Cooper

COOPER, Alice

Vince Furnier, aka Alice Cooper, shocked parents worldwide with lurid make-up and a bizarre stage act. Following UK smashes School's Out and Elected the band split up in 1974 . Cooper still daubs on the black eye make up for occasional stage appearances but is most happy living in Paradise Valley, Arizona where he plays golf off a handicap of five. In 1996 he contributed a version of the Herod song for the new recording of Jesus Christ Superstar.

Drummer Neal Smith went into property in New England; Guitarist Michael Bruce became a student detention councillor in Arizona and wrote a book about the band called No More Mr Nice Guy, named after one of their hits; Dennis Dunnaway (bass) bought an arts and crafts shop with his wife; Glen Buxton (guitar) returned to Iowa where he has since struggled with drink and drugs problems.

CRAMER, Floyd

Once referred to as the best country pianist in the world whose On the Rebound reached No. 1 in the early Sixties. Twenty years later he returned to prominence by writing the theme to the television series Dallas. Now living and working as a session musician back in his Nashville base.
On the Rebound (1961).

CREAM

Supergroup comprising of Eric Clapton, Jack Bruce and Ginger Baker who split in 1968 after performing a brilliant farewell concert - which produced a Goodbye album and TV movie. Clapton and Baker formed Blind Faith then Baker became interested in African music and opened a recording studio in Nigeria where Wings recorded Band on the Run. In the late Seventies Baker went into semi-retirement, ran an olive farm in Italy for most of the Eighties and now lives in Parker, Colorado where he is registered as one of the town's firemen. In 1993 the trio got together again briefly to perform in Los Angeles. Then in 1994 Bruce and Baker combined with Gary Moore for a project under the banner of M.
I Feel Free (1966).

CREEDENCE CLEARWATER REVIVAL

Tom Fogerty left at the turn of the Seventies to embark on a solo career . They continued to perform as a threesome until 1972 when Cook and Clifford joined the Don Harrison Band. Fogerty recorded one album as the Blue Ridge Rangers. Band members re-formed under the name of Creedence Clearwater Revisited until their ex-colleague John Fogerty gained an injunction preventing the use of the name – they have since toured as Cosmos Factory. Fogerty himself has been the centre of several court battles with his former record label, firstly to be released from his contract, then the label's boss Saul Zaentz tried unsuccessfully to sue Fogerty for $142million claiming he had been slandered by tracks Mr Greed and Zantz Kant Danz on Fogerty's albums Proud Mary and Bad Moon Rising. Fogerty died of respiratory failure in 1990.

CROCE, Jim

Killed in a plane crash in 1973 at the peak of his career. Bad Bad Leroy Brown had been an American number one before his death and this achievement was matched posthumously when Time In a Bottle again hit the top spot following its use in the film The Last American Hero.

CROSBY, Bing

Mr White Christmas died on 14th October 1977, while on a Madrid golf course after a lifetime of musical achievement.

Boy George and Helen Terry

CROSBY, STILLS & NASH & YOUNG

Crosby, Stills and Nash are alive and well – just! – Dave Crosby (formerly of the Byrds) having undergone a liver transplant in 1994. He has now fully recovered and the trio made an emotional appearance at Kent State University in 1997 as part of tribute to the four students killed by National Guardsmen on the same spot 27 years earlier when the band were in their Marrakesh Express phase. Such is their success they are now preparing to go public on the US Stock Market in similar vein to David Bowie's recent listing. (See also NEIL YOUNG).

CRUSH, Bobby

Opportunity Knocks talent show winner whose cheesy grin should have given us warning of what was to come! He went on to write the equally corny Orville's Song for Keith Harris and sidekick. Now an actor who recently starred as an unlikely Frank N Furter in the Rocky Horror Show.

CRYSTALS

Formed in 1961 but it was Phil Spector who became their mentor and inspiration by providing Da Doo Ron Ron in 1963. In 1992 singer Darlene Love appeared as Danny Glover's wife in the film Lethal Weapon while original member DD Kennibrew has put together a new version of the Crystals to tour.

CULTURE CLUB

Boy George's group broke up in 1986 allowing him a solo number one with Everything I Own (previously a Ken Boothe reggae chart-topper in 1974). Since then the flamboyant singer has overcome a brush with drug addiction; joined the Hare Krishna movement in 1991; upset all and sundry with his autobiography Take It Like A Man; and become an acclaimed Club disc jockey. Helen Terry, who provided the female voice on Church Of The Poison Mind now works behind the scenes in television on TV coverage of The Brits and producing music documentaries about musical artists. *Karma Chameleon (1983).*

CUTTING CREW

(I Just) Died In Your Arms paved the way for a brief run of chart entries in the late Eighties for Cutting Crew. Nick Van Eade, the group's guitarist is now compiling a book entitled So You Want To Be A Songwriter from his home recording studio near Gatwick, Sussex. His three former colleagues still make their living from music with Kevin MacMichael working from home in Nova Scotia in his native Canada.

DACTYL, Terry & The Dinosaurs

Also known as Brett Marvin & The Thunderbolts but chose to use the Dactyl name for their Jonathan King assisted single Seaside Shuffle which reached No. 2 in 1972 as they didn't want to put their hard core fans off. Singer and keyboard player Jona Lewie later achieved solo hits with Kitchen At Parties and Stop The Cavalry.

DALE, Jim

With an eternally youthful face, familiar on stage both here and in America, remarkably it is now forty years since Dale was a star in the charts. A regular in the Carry On film series until 1970, he then took to the boards starring as Barnum in the States and as Fagin in Oliver at the London Palladium in 1996. His daredevil spirit which led to tightrope walking across a canyon has earned him an honorary membership to The Association Of Hollywood Stuntmen.
Be My Girl (1957).

DAMNED

Captain Sensible left the band in 1984 to enjoy solo success with his single Happy Talk. The band continued and in 1986 they hit No. 3 in England with Eloise. In 1989 the group briefly split again, having done so previously in 1978 then re-united again in 1991. They are still led by Dave Vanian and with Captain Sensible back in the fold. Drummer Rat Scabies spent a time living and writing in Huntingdon Beach, America before returning home to briefly work as a Food and Restaurant critic. The magazine he worked for folded allowing him time to concentrate on his dubiously named band Dog Exercise Area.

DANA

It was in 1970 that Dana first broke through to world-wide success. Representing Ireland and singing All Kinds Of Everything, she ran away with the international votes to win the

Jim Dale

Dana

Eurovision Song Contest. As well as continuing with live performances she broke new ground when her first book Dana – An Autobiography was published in 1985. Now based in America, Dana has fulfilled a life long ambition by recording Gospel albums and was invited to sing for Pope John Paul when he visited Denver in 1993. She has also shown an interest in politics and ran for President in her native Ireland in 1997.
All Kinds Of Everything (1970).

DANNY & THE JUNIORS

At The Hop still captures the image of American high school dances of the Fifties and has continued to provide a living for several of the original Juniors. Danny (Danny Rapp) died in April 1983 having apparently shot himself but the band decided to carry on, now fronted by Joe Terranova.

DARBY, Terence Trent

Java Records, an independent Los Angeles label, intends releasing a new album for Darby's long-awaited comeback. The American singer's run of chart success dried up in 1993 after eight top twenty entries including Sign Your Name which reached No. 2 in 1988.

DARIN, Bobby

Splish Splash and Dream Lover are arguably how most people remember Bobby Darin. However, he also managed to establish himself as a successful actor and one of America's most popular night club entertainers before his death from a heart attack in the Lebanon in 1973. Darin was only 37 at the time but had suffered from heart disease since a childhood bout of rheumatic fever.

DARTS

Funtime rockers who had a string of hits following their explosion into the charts in 1977 with debut single Daddy Cool. By the Eighties their brand of mayhem had lost its chart appeal. Frontman Den Hegarty later scored a minor success with Voodoo Voodoo before turning his attention to presenting children's television programmes. He later studied for a degree in psychology after he had a car crash and his house had burnt down forcing him to review his life. This has led to him working one day a week at his local Citizens Advice Bureau. Rita Ray (Lydia Murdoch) co-ran and was a DJ at Mambo Inn club in Brixton's Loughborough Hotel pub. Thump Thompson bought a West London flower shop and writes books. John Dummer suffered a nervous breakdown and now lives in France where he bought, refurbished and sold a monastery. Bob Fish spent a time painting murals in millionaire's houses in Spain but is now back in the UK working as a graphic designer.
Daddy Cool (1977).

DAVID & JONATHAN

Otherwise known as Roger Cook and Roger Greenaway this formidable writing team providing hits for The Fortunes, Andy Williams and the New Seekers. Their first hit was Michelle, penned by the Beatles. In the Seventies they became part of Blue Mink.

DAVIS, Billie

First entered the chart in 1962 in a duet with Mike Sarne with Will I What but gained more publicity for her public romance with Jet Harris of the Shadows. She is still performing and is particularly popular in Spain.
Tell Him (1963).

Sammy Davis Jr

Own Studio

Ten who can record in comfort

1   Dave Pegg (Fairport Convention)
2   Jose Feliciano
3   Sonny (Sonny & Cher)
4   Midge Ure
5   Captain & Tennille
6   Ginger Baker (Cream)
7   George Young & Harry Vanda (Easybeats)
8   Johnny Nash
9   Jive Bunny
10 Lobo

DAVIS Sammy Jr

One of the true entertainers, one-eyed Davis was singer, instrumentalist and dancer. Died in May 1990.

SPENCER DAVIS GROUP

Formed in 1963 and had close to a dozen top ten hits. In 1967 Steve Winwood left the group to form Traffic and then the ill-fated supergroup Blind Faith. His brother Muff followed and joined Chris Blackwell at Island Records, for whom he later became an executive. Today Muff is head of S2 Records (part of Columbia) and has been behind the scenes for 18 years. In 1969 Spencer Davis disbanded the group and moved to America's West Coast to work as a consultant for a video production company. Fluent in French German and Spanish and the holder of a degree in Modern Languages, he had originally given up his teaching career to take up music. By the mid Seventies he was an executive at Island Records and then became head of A& R for independent Hollywood label. 1995 saw him tour with his European Spencer Davis Group joined by original member Peter York. He has since starred in television adverts, the hit series Married With Children and became co-host of TV show Desert Rock TV. Davis now utilises skills from his former career to deliver lectures about the music business and claims to be having more fun than he ever did.

Keep On Running (1965).

DAWN

Led by Tony Orlando Dawn topped the British charts in 1971 with Knock Three Times – two years before their greatest triumph – Tie A Yellow Ribbon Round The Old Oak Tree which went on to become an anthem for many good causes. When the trio split in 1977 Thelma Hopkins embarked on a TV acting career. Orlando has since encountered several personal difficulties, his sister died, and one of his best friends committed suicide, resulting in many months of therapy. In the 1980s he turned to acting, and stood in for Jim Dale in Barnum on Broadway. In 1989 Tony Orlando and Dawn re-united although Hopkins also continued her acting career starring in the ABC TV series Family Matters. In 1991 Orlando wrote a song for the troops taking part in Operation Desert Storm but the conflict ended before it could be released.

DAY, Doris

The Fifties film star also enjoyed an equally successful career as a singer. A string of top films and ten top ten records should have set Day up for life. However, it was not until she won a court case against her lawyer that she finally received most of the $20 million he was claimed to have embezzled. Lives in Carmel, California and owns the Spanish style hotel Cypress Inn and heads the Doris Day Animal League.

Dead or Alive

DEAD OR ALIVE

Fronted by glam gender bender Pete Burns, they are still best known for their 1985 hit You Spin Me Round. Now led by Burns and Steve Guy, they are incredibly popular in Japan and in 1995 sold half a million copies of their album The New Kleapatra.

Dozy, Beaky, Mick & Titch

DAVE DEE, DOZY, BEAKY, MICK & TITCH

Fronted by former Policeman Dave Dee the band from Wiltshire were the biggest selling act in the UK in 1967. Their combination of music, comedy and theatre on stage earned them a string of top ten hits such as Hold Tight; Bend It; Zabadak; and their only No. 1 The Legend of Xanadu which featured Dees whip cracking to maximum effect. Dee briefly pursued a solo career before finally swapping his whip for a record company desk at Warner Brothers and then forming his own record label, Double D Records. He now performs live with fellow sixties stars Marmalade.

Dozy; Beaky; Tich and Mick, eventually returned to their Salisbury roots having spent two years entertaining the rich and famous in Marbella on The Costa Del Sol. John Dymond (Beaky) became a painter and decorator. Ian Amey (Tich) runs a nursing home and plays in a new version of the band with Trevor Davies (Dozy). Finally, the original drummer now runs his own driving school – The Mick Wilson School Of Motoring.

DEAN, Jimmy

Had an American hit in 1961 with Big Bad John. His own brand of country music is still an attraction on the club circuit.

DEE, Kiki

Despite being the first white British artist to win a recording contract with Tamla Motown, Dee only achieved mainstream success after her switch to Elton John's Rocket Label. Under his guidance Amoureuse and I've Got The Music In Me reached the top twenty but it was Don't Go Breaking My Heart ,a duet with mentor Elton, that finally hit No. 1 in 1976. Dee now shares her time between music and theatre having appeared on stage in Willy Russell's Blood Brothers.

DEEP PURPLE

Along with Black Sabbath have represented the best of British heavy metal for almost thirty years. Roger Glover, Ian Paice, Ian Gillan and Jon Lord still perform and command the same fanatical following. They released Purpendicular in 1996 and are recording a new studio album in Orlando, Florida. Former members David Coverdale and Ritchie Blackmore continue to front their own successful outfits, Whitesnake and Ritchie Blackmore's Rainbow. American guitarist Tommy Bolin joined in 1975 but died from a heroin overdose in Miami in 1976 shortly after the bands dissolution. Gillan is now a qualified scuba diving instructor and holds an Armenian Medal of Honour. He quit

Ian Gillian of
Deep Purple

Comin' Home. The bubble burst in 1972 when they split – privately and professionally and divorced. In 1976 it was reported that Bonnie went into a field with a shotgun to commit suicide but had a change of heart. In 1988 she featured in the TV series Fame, has appeared in Roseanne and in the film about The Doors. Since then both have continued to record separately as session musicians.

DELLS

American vocal group who although massively successful in their homeland only breached the British charts once – in 1969 with a medley I Can Sing A Rainbow – Love Is Blue. The film The Five Heartbeats was based on their lives and careers and they still work the club circuit in the States.

both the band and the music industry in 1973 to concentrate on a variety of private business interests including an hotel anda motorbike manufacturing concern. Returning in 1976 he first formed the Ian Gillan Band, then joined Black Sabbath before Purple reunited in 1984. Having left again he rejoined in 1993 in time for their 25th anniversary. To add to all of this he has had a book of poetry published, written his autobiography Child In Time and penned a film screenplay.
Smoke On The Water (1977).

DEES, Rick
And His Cast Of Idiots

Memphis Disc Jockey who cocked a snoop at the disco boom with his Disco Duck which then ironically caught on in the dance halls. After experiencing a world wide hit he returned to the comfort of radio where he hosts a show on KIIS in Los Angeles.

DEKKER, Desmond

Originally from Jamaica, Dekker became the first Jamaican to score a No. 1 in England with his song The Israelites in 1969. He was declared bankrupt in 1985 but since 1993 he has been a popular draw in cabaret.
The Israelites (1969).

DELANEY and BONNIE

Delaney (Bramlett) and Bonnie married within seven days of meeting in 1967. Their only British chart single success was with

John Denver

DENVER, John

Born John Deutschendorf and later changed his name. Wrote Leaving on a Jet Plane for Peter, Paul and Mary but best known for Annies Song (1974) and a host of easy listening folk ballads. His Greatest Hits album sold over 10million copies. Became an active environmentalist and died when his light plane crashed into the sea off the Californian coast.

DENVER, Karl

In the early Sixties scored with Wimoweh and

now living in Manchester and regularly performing in cabaret(especially in Spain). In 1990 he formed an unlikely liaison with fellow Mancunians the Happy Mondays. Their joint effort Lazyitis – One Armed Boxer scraped into the top 50 some twenty six years after his last hit.

DEREK & THE DOMINOES

Formed by Eric Clapton, post-Cream and part of the web of supergroups through which Clapton has travelled.
Layla (a hit in 1972, 1982, 1992).

DEXYS MIDNIGHT RUNNERS

Formed in 1978 and fronted by the enigmatic Kevin Rowland. Hits like Geno and Come On Eileen should have set Rowland up for life, however the past few years have not been the best for Rowland – signing on the dole, house re-possession, court appearances and personal problems; the only highlight was meeting up with a daughter lost some 20 years ago. In 1991 he was declared bankrupt but has since re-emerged as a solo artist despite confessing that he pinched the ideas and resulting Dexys glory from a friend.

Karl Denver

Bo Diddley

DIDDLEY, Bo

Bo Diddley was responsible for writing many R & B classics including Road-Runner, I'm A Man, and Who Do You Love. Latterly he has toured with Ron Wood as The Gunslingers and formed a surprising touring partner with the Clash. In 1994, financial rewards caught up with his undoubted success when he was awarded $400,000 by a Los Angeles judge presiding over his claim for backdated royalties.

DION

Dion's biggest British hit's were Runaround Sue and The Wanderer – since covered by Racey (1980) and Status Quo (1984). In 1973, thirteen years after their first split, he re-formed The Belmonts for a reunion concert at Madison Square Garden. A growing interest in blues music dominated his later musical output but he also became tangled with drugs. When he finally kicked his heroin habit, Dion became a devout born again Christian releasing a number of religious albums and remains a popular live act.

DIXIE-CUPS

Original members Barbara Ann Hawkins and her sister Rosa-Lee are still performing their famous Sixties songs like Chapel Of Love and Iko Iko to appreciative audiences throughout the States.

DOBSON, Anita

Reached No. 4 in 1986 with Anyone Can Fall In Love to the theme tune of Eastenders while starring as Angie, landlady of the Old Vic. Dobson, whose other half is ex-Queen guitarist Brian May, has since starred on stage in Leave Him To Heaven and Budgie and regularly pops up on our TV screens, most recently in the series Dangerfield.

DOCTOR AND THE MEDICS

Originally formed to win a £5 bet for top club DJ Steve McGuire (The Doctor - so named after he failed to gain entry into Medical College). He and original member Colette Anadin still create a party atmosphere wherever they play live. Vom (drummer) moved to Germany and has just signed to RCA records with a band called The Armageddon Dildos! Wendi Anadin left the band and is mother to the Doctor's three children. Colette Anadin also works as a body double for Gwyneth Paltrow and Uma Therman (most recently in The Avengers). Steve McGuire co-owns Halcyon Production, a company with a fleet of vehicles used for transporting bands around the world. The Doctor started his own snail farm in the Brecon Beacons but this abruptly ended in 1991 when his entire stock of 50,000 snails died . He has since formed a record label

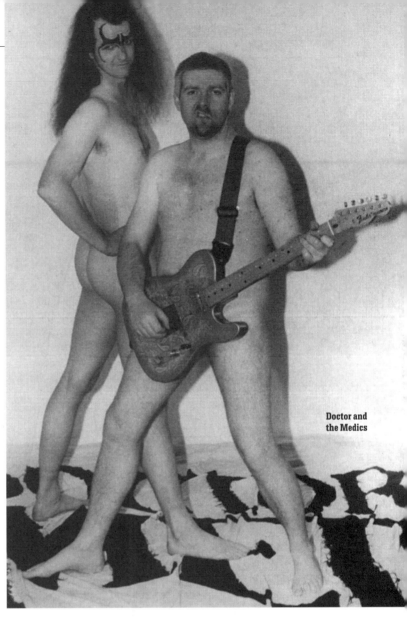

Doctor and the Medics

called Madman Records with McGuire and has been known to act as a 'Motivational Therapist and Healer'!
Spirit In The Sky (1986).

DR FEELGOOD

The Southend based pub-rockers have continued to perform despite the departure of guitarist Wilko Johnson and the death of lead singer Lee Brilleaux who died of throat cancer in Canvey Island in 1994. The band celebrated their 25th anniversary with the release of a double CD and biography on their own record label Grand Records and still perform live. Johnson teamed up with ex-

Dr Feelgood

Blockhead Norman Watt-Roy twelve years ago and they have since recorded three albums and play up to 100 gigs a year. Former Feelgood Gypie Mayo joined the New Yardbirds for their 1997 American tour.
Milk and Alcohol (1979).

Dr Hook

DR HOOK

Despite being a cult band who had performed on the road for fifteen years, at one stage the band was bankrupt and were only saved by the success of their later songs When You're In love With A Beautiful Woman and Sexy Eyes. The singer with the eyepatch, Ray Sawyer, left in the Eighties to become a session singer in Nashville and the other front man Dennis Lacorriere (guitarist) went solo but is now songwriting, also in Nashville. A new version of the band continues to perform, with Sawyer back to be the only original member. Drummer John Christ produces for artists including Whitney Houston and Diana Ross.
Sylvia's Mother (1972).

DODD, Ken

Singer, rib-tickler and leader of the Diddymen hit the headlines following court action bought against him unsuccessfully by the Inland Revenue. Now lives in Knotty Ash with former Bluebell dancer Anne Jones and their Poodle called Doodle!
Tears (1965).

DOLBY, Thomas

Born Thomas Morgan Robertson, the son of a famous archaeologist listed in Who's Who, Thomas Dolby is reputed to have made a deal with the other Tom Robinson that whoever achieved success first would use the name. Having come a close second Dolby managed to climb the charts twice with Hyperactive, firstly in 1984 and again ten years later. Now lives in Los Angeles with his actress wife Kathleen Beller (Kirby Colby in TVs Dynasty), where he makes his living as a writer and is heavily involved in multimedia projects.

DOLLAR

Poppy boy girl duo comprising of David Van Day and Thereze Bazaar. Van Day lives in Brighton and now performs with Bucks Fizz. A reunion in 1987 produced a return to the charts with 'O'l'Amour. Bazaar then moved to Australia and opened a jewellery shop in Sydney together with her sister.
Love Gotta Hold On Me (1979).

DOMINO, Fats

Ain't That A Shame, Poor Me, Please Leave Me and All By Myself released between 1954 to 1959 all sold between an incredible three

Fats Domino

and five million copies! In the Sixties Fats reduced his recording work load and went into semi-retirement. In 1972 he appeared in the movie Let The Good Times Roll. He now lives in New Orleans.
Blueberry Hill (1956).

DONEGAN, Lonnie

Skiffle superstar whose My Old Man's A Dustman (which in 1960 entered the British hit parade at Number 1) sold three million copies worldwide but he received just £5 as a session fee for making the record. Branched out in showbusiness and became an all-round entertainer. Then in 1976 he suffered three major heart attacks in rapid succession which curtailed his performing.

Thomas Dolby

Disc Jockeys

Ten DJs who have entered the charts

1 Rick Dees
2 Pat & Mick
3 Laurie Lingo
4 Tony Blackburn
5 Terry Wogan
6 Steve Wright
7 Jimmy Young
8 Kenny Everett
9 Alexis Korner
10 Wink Martindale

Lonnie Donnegan

He later made his home in California but still spends three months each year in England where Donegan plays the occasional live date.

DONALDSON, Bo & The Heywoods

Had an American No. 1 with their version of Paper Lace's Billy Dont be a Hero in 1974. Bo Heywood now sells alarms in Los Angeles.

DONOVAN

As much a part of the Swinging Sixties as Carnaby Street and Mary Quant, Donovan emerged as juke boxes throughout the country echoed the sound of his Mellow Yellow, Jennifer Juniper and Hurdy Gurdy Man. As the decade drew to a close so did his career and he walked away from the industry and its associated trappings of wealth. He rested in a quiet cottage in England before settling near Joshua Tree in the California desert for many recuperative years. A revived (in every sense) Donovan has now emerged with new energy and enthusiasm to live performances.

DONOVAN Jason

Aussie soap star of Neighbours who ventured into pop music with Stock Aitken and Waterman to twice top the charts in 1989. Starred in West End Musicals then withdrew from the public eye amid rumours of ill health.

DOOBIE BROTHERS

Patrick Simmonds, Mike MacDonald and Tom Johnson are three original members who still perform under the group's title. One of their former drummers, Bobby Lakind, suffered from inoperable brain cancer and died at the age of 47 in 1992. John Hartman left the group and became a fireman and a part-time policeman but was turned down to become a full-time police officer on the grounds that he lied about the full extent of his drug use.
Listen to the Music (1974).

DOORS

Now buried in the same Paris cemetery as Oscar Wilde, Edith Piaf and Chopin, singer Jim Morrison died from a heart attack in 1971. The Doors played on with Riders On The

Donovan

Jason Donovan then and now

Storm becoming a chart success later that year. In 1973 they split up for good with Ray Manzarek concentrating on production after several solo projects. In 1991 Oliver Stone made a film about the band which triggered a revival, resulting in greater record sales than in their Sixties heyday. Despite this, Manzarek was not impressed, claiming that Stone was a nice man but a bad film-maker. Robbie Kreiger has taken to painting and together with his former keyboard player has given approval to an official Doors Website on the internet. This has apparently registered over 200,000 hits in its first year proving that interest in the band is still as strong in the 1990s.

DORSEY, Lee

Boxer known as Kid Chocolate who turned singer and turned Working In The Coalmine into a top 10 hit on both sides of the Atlantic. In 1970 he returned to his New Orleans birthplace to spend more time running his car repair shop. He also managed to tour including a stint supporting the Clash in 1980. Died from emphysema in 1986.

DOUBLE TROUBLE

Rapper Michael Menson died in 1989 aged 29. He had been attacked by a gang of youths, soaked in petrol and set alight. The group's only top ten hit was achieved later that year and was appropriately called Street Tuff.

DOUGLAS, Carl

In 1974 the nation's fascination with badly dubbed Bruce Lee films allowed Douglas to score a No. 1 hit with the tongue in cheek Kung Fu Fighting. He still makes regular cabaret performances (thankfully now minus the ridiculous Japanese headgear) on the back of Seventies revivals and royalties from the self-penned tune have ensured a

comfortable existence for the larger than life singer ever since.

DOUGLAS, Craig

Had a No. 1 with Sam Cooke's Only Sixteen in 1959 and is still performing in cabaret.

DRAKE, Charlie

My Boomerang Won't Come Back and Mr Custer summed up Drakes' cheeky chappy screen and stage image. He admitted to having lost all his wealth through gambling, but recently re-emerged (minus the habit) in appropriate surroundings, starring in Jim Davidson's Sinderella.

Carl
Douglas

Craig Douglas

Charlie Drake (and friends!)

DRIFTERS

25 years on from first release and 200million record sales since, the Drifters still perform regularly although the original line up had disappeared even before they released the now standards Stand By Me and Up On The Roof. In fact, by the mid-Seventies there were at least 40 ex-Drifters and at one time there were a many as 10 rival bands playing at the same time on the cabaret circuit. Three of the original members have now died; Rudy Lewis passed away in 1963; Ellsbury Hobbs died of cancer in May 1996 at the age of 60; Clyde McPhatter died in 1972 as a result of a serious drug and alcohol addiction.

The most successful former Drifter, Ben E King, returned to the top of the UK chart in 1986 with Stand By Me following the release of the film of the same name.
Save The Last Dance For Me (1960).

DRIVER 67

In 1978 the romantic troubles of a brummie taxi driver provided an improbable Christmas hit in the shape of the novelty song Car 67. The cabbie involved – Paul Phillip – hadn't been in music previously and never troubled the charts again. He is now a successful publisher whose magazines include Video Trade Weekly and the popular black music weekly Echoes.

DUNDAS, David

Lord David Dundas, son of the Marquess of Zetland, shed his noble gladrags to achieve a 1976 top ten with Jeans On. The song had been popularised by a Brutus jeans television advertising campaign. Dundas now earns his crust as a composer and film score writer and ironically his credits include the film How To Get Ahead In Advertising.
Jeans On (1976).

DUNN, Clive

The actor better known as Corporal Jones in Dad's Army, Dunn topped the British charts in 1970 with the sentimental Grandad. Gave up life in Britain to run a cafe under the Mediterranean sun in Portugal.

DUPREE, Simon & Their Big Sound

Formed in Portsmouth by brothers Derek and Ray Shulman they had a hit in the hippy era with Kites which reached the top ten in 1967. Two years later the group disbanded when Derek suffered a nervous breakdown. After a period of recovery he was re-united with his brother in the newly formed Gentle Giant and they were also joined by third brother Phil.

Duran Duran

DURAN DURAN

Founder members Simon Le Bon and Nick Rhodes lead today's Duran Duran who provided Out Of My Mind for Val Kilmer's 1996 film The Saint.

They are aided by Warren Cuccurullo who replaced Andy Taylor when he left to record a solo album in 1986. Taylor and his brother John had taken a sabbatical two years earlier to team up with Robert Palmer as the Power Station. John Taylor finally announced his departure from the group during an acoustic set performed at the 1997 Durancon, a gathering of the group's fans. Simon Le Bon and Nick Rhodes continued the New Romantics theme into their private lives by both marrying models. Le Bon took up sailing and was airlifted to safety after his yacht Drum overturned during a race. *Girls On Film (1981).*

DURY, Ian & Blockheads

Despite suffering from Polio since childhood Ian Dury has enjoyed a full musical career which started with pub band Kilburn and the High Roads in the early Seventies. In 1973 he was able to give up his art teaching job at Canterbury Art College to concentrate full time on music.

He formed the Blockheads and their New Boots and Panties album sold in excess of one million copies. Reasons to be Cheerful and Hit Me With Your Rhythm Stick also topped the charts in 1979. Micky Gallagher (the band's pianist) collabrated with Dury on a musical called Apples which Dury also starred in. Charlie Charles, the groups drummer, died in 1990 of cancer. Dury also does TV work and has hosted late night show Metro as well as apperaring in a number of other roles.

DYLAN, Bob

The son of a Jewish shop-keeper who became one of the most influential singer-songwriters ever. Now well into his fifties Dylan is still performing both as a solo artist and as part of the Travelling Wilburys. He deigned to appear at Woodstock 1994 having turned down the 1969 festival whilst in his heyday. His last chart entry in the UK was twenty years ago but he still commands huge audiences by virtue of his legendary status. In 1997 he shook fans worldwide when he was hospitalised with heart problems and was forced to call off live performances. *The Times They Are A Changin' (1965).*

EARTH, WIND & FIRE

This nine piece band still are still touring the globe with their blend of African and big band music. Philip Bailey had a 1985 solo No. 1 in Britain with Easy Lover. Both he and founder member Maurice White have become acclaimed producers working with stars like Neil Diamond. The current line up includes former Temptations member Sheldon Reynolds, but in 1997 White retired from the road whilst denying rumours of poor health.

Sheena Easton

EASTON, Sheena

Sheena Easton's current Hollywood lifestyle is a far cry from more humble beginnings when she was discovered by Esther Rantzen's TV programme The Big Time in 1980. She has lived in America for the past fifteen years and in 1990 vowed never to return to Scotland after bottles were thrown at her at a concert. Her acting career has blossomed and she has appeared in Miami Vice, the film Indecent Proposal, and on the Broadway stage in Grease, as well as providing the voice for Sacha in All Dogs Go To Heaven.

EASTWOOD, Clint

Former lumberjack who became Mayor of Carmel, California, where he now owns a restaurant called the Hog's Breath Inn! Dirty Harry shot into the top twenty with his rendition of I Talk To The Trees in 1970. It was on the flip side of Lee Marvin's Wanderin Star.

EASYBEATS

After a massive smash with Friday On My Mind guitarists Harry Vanda and George Young moved back to Australia although they did make a further chart appearance in 1983 as A Flash in the Pan with Waiting For A Train which reached No. 7 in the UK .They went on to produce AC/DC whose line up includes Young's two brothers and open their own recording studio which was responsible for the success of John Paul Young. Lead singer Steve Wright still tours as the Easybeats. *Friday On My Mind (1966).*

EDDY, Duane

Rock and roll guitarist with his own original sound who has sold more than 30 million records from nearly 25 single successes. In Britain alone he has clocked up 21 hits. He reappeared into the charts in 1986 with Art Of Noise performing Peter Gunn and at the age of 59 is still twanging his guitar.

EDELMAN, Randy

Uptown Uptempo Woman and Concrete And Clay, both hits in 1976, established Edelmans credentials as a solo performer. He is now a leading writer of soundtracks for films; his credits include Parenthood and Kindergarten Cop. He also has the distinction of being responsible for the theme tune to the TV cartoon series The Care Bears!

EDISON LIGHTHOUSE

See BROTHERHOOD OF MAN & WHITE PLAINS.

Artists

Ten who are handy with the brush

1. Mags Furuholmen (A-Ha)
2. Herb Alpert
3. Tony Bennett
4. Bob Fish (Darts)
5. Richie Havens
6. Syd Barrett (Pink Floyd)
7. Mason Williams
8. Ron Wood
9. David Bowie
10. Captain Beefheart

EDMUNDS, Dave

I Hear You Knocking sold over three million copies and stayed at No. 1 for over three months. He is now living in Los Angeles and has produced artists such as The Everly Brothers and Status Quo and also contributed songs to Steve Martin's film Planes, Trains and Automobiles.

Eighth Wonder

EIGHTH WONDER

The band which included Patsy Kensit and her brother scored four top twenty hits in the Eighties. While Patsy lives the high life as Mrs Oasis Gallagher, Jamie, who was also a one time pin up now lives in a flat in Clerkenwell and is a registered heroin addict.

ELECTRIC LIGHT ORCHESTRA

After eight years of hits, ELO finally had their first No. 1 (in conjunction with Olivia Newton-John) with Xanadu in 1980. In 1983 lead singer Jeff Lynne began a career as a producer for artists such as Tom Jones, George Harrison and the Beatles. He is also one of the Travelling Wilburys, although a dispute with his record label Warner Brothers has halted the release of his second solo alum and the third Wilburys offering. Bev Bevan, the group's drummer missed the buzz of live gigs and is now touring and recording with his own band ELO Part II who include several of the old band as well as those who joined the group OrKestra, formed after Jeff Lynne disbanded ELO in 1986.

ELLINGTON, Duke

Considered to be one of the best band leaders ever, Ellington died from cancer in May 1974. His son Mercer has since taken over at the helm.

ELLIS, Shirley

Retired from the music business in 1967 two years after her most famous hit The Clapping Song scaled the British chart. The same tune provided a top twenty success for The Belle Stars in 1982. Shirley now lives in New York.

EMERSON, LAKE & PALMER

Famous for extravagant stage shows, Emerson, Lake and Palmer consisted of Keith Emerson (ex-Nice) on keyboards, Greg Lake (ex-King Crimson) on bass and Carl Palmer (ex-Atomic Rooster) on drums. Formed in 1970, the band officially broke up in 1978 and

ELO

Emerson and Lake (right) in 1996

t took thirteen years for a serious reunion to happen. In that time Emerson wrote several film scores, Lake formed a band with Gary Moore and Palmer joined supergroup Asia. They even played in every combination as a duo but never again as the original trio. In 1991 a brief reunion ended when Emerson needed treatment on one of his hands. He has since completed a musical score, tunes for the Iron Man cartoon in US where he lives and written his as yet unpublished autobiography tentatively titled Pictures. Following a tour of Japan and America there is finally hope that 1997 will see them return to the British stage over 25 years after their explosion on to the rock scene at the Isle Of Wight Festival. They have re-launched Manticore (their own record label) to release a recording of their second ever gig– the IOW Festival.
Fanfare For Common Man (1977).

EMERY, Dick

TV Entertainer Of The Year in 1972, Emery had an early hit with If You Love Her but it was not until 1973 when You Are Awful charted on the back of his film of the same name.
Oh, You Are Awful (But I Like You) (1973).

EQUALS

The founder members are still touring without former singer Eddie Grant but they are sill linked to him through Grant's Ice record label.
Baby Come Back (1968).

ESSEX, David

Able to adapt to either acting or singing, David Essex took a sabbatical in 1992 to teach drama and music at a teacher training college. He also spent two years as president of the Voluntary Service Overseas. In 1994 his revival of Buddy Holly's True Love Ways with Catherine Zeta Jones scraped into the British charts. In 1997 a new cover version of his Rock On topped the American charts while his own album scaled the British charts. He also became involved in writing a Ballet score for a performance of Beauty and the Beast at the Royal Albert Hall.

EURYTHMICS

Annie Lennox and Dave Stewart were linked both romantically and musically in the guise of The Tourists from 1977 to 1980 (I Only Want To Be With You, a No. 4 in 1979). When both broke up they formed a new relationship as The

David Essex

Eurythmics and scored six successive top ten singles before There Musty Be An Angel went all the way to the top. In 1981 Stewart suffered a re-occurrence of lung problems, Lennox suffered a nervous breakdown, and the group finally split in 1983. Dave Stewart is now producer, song writer, video director and film maker. His most recent success being the guidance of Alishas Attic to stardom. Annie Lennox meanwhile has pursued a quieter solo career but has not toured since and makes only a handful of live appearances. A new album is now being planned for 1998 release.

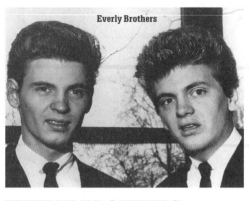

Everly Brothers

EVERLY BROTHERS

Don and Phil were one of the most successful vocal duos in pop music during the latter days of the 1950s and early 1960s. In 1963 while on tour of Britain, Don Everly suffered a nervous breakdown and Phil was forced to carry on alone. It marked a major turning point in their career. From then on they gradually went their own separate ways. Don returned to Nashville to carve a career for himself in the country field and in 1990 his daughter Erin married Guns n Roses lead singer Axel Rose in Las Vegas. Since their reunion at the Albert Hall in 1983, they have continued to tour but still find time to run an annual festival and perform benefit concerts for worthy causes including their own Everly Brothers Foundation. A statue of the Everly Brothers is erected at City Hall, Central City in their home state of Kentucky.
Bye Bye Love (1957).

FABIAN
Reverted to real name Fabian Forte for a career in acting but still tours with The Boys Of Bandstand with Frankie Avalon and Bobby Rydell.
Hound Dog Man (1960).

FAIRPORT CONVENTION
Five original members are still doing the rounds and were joined by former members at the 1997 Cropredy Festival and recorded a new album due out on Woodworm Records. Dave Pegg also worked with Jethro Tull and now runs Woodworm and the Woodworm Studio. Ric Sanders (ex- Soft Machine) collaborated with Jools Holland on an educational video about the violin. Dave Mattacks(drummer) joined in 1969 and also owns one of the largest snare drum collections in the world. Sandy Denny died in 1978. In mid-Seventies Richard Thompson announced he was going to live in a commune but returned to recording and live work within a couple of years and since 1978 has released at least one album every year.

FAIRWEATHER-LOW, Andy
Guitarist and singer, for full details see AMEN CORNER.

FAITH, Adam
The rock n roll gladrags have now been exchanged for pinstripe suits as Adam Faith pop singer has been transformed into financial advisor and businessman. Acting roles have dotted the route, appearing as Budgie on TV in the Seventies and on the West End stage in the Nineties, while film credits have included Stardust and McVicar.

Adam Faith

Marianne Faithfull then and now (right)

FAITHFULL, Marianne

A real Sixties child whose autobiography Faithfull was published in 1996 chronicling a turbulent private life littered with drugs and suicide bids. Mick Jagger's former girlfriend was back in London in 1997, breaking away from her peaceful Irish hideaway to perform An Evening in the Wiemar Republic. *As Tears Go By (1964).*

FAME, Georgie

By 1968 Fame had notched up three number ones, two with his Blueflames and The Ballard Of Bonnie and Clyde with former Animal Alan Price. As well as still performing as a popular jazz keyboard player, he has been a member of Van Morrison's backing band since the early Nineties.

FAMILY

Family split in 1973. Chapman and Charlie Whitney (the guitarist who wrote most of the group's songs) continued together as The Street Walkers. Then Chapman went to follow a solo path. Jim Cregan who joined the band in 1972 and went on to have success with Cockney Rebel before joining Rod Stewart's band. He also married Linda Lewis. Grech quit to join Blind Faith in 1971 but died from kidney and liver failure following a brain haemorrhage in 1990. Tony Ashton, who had also joined in 1972, and Rob Townsend (drummer) formed Medicine Head.

FARLOWE, Chris

Although still performing, Farlowe can normally be found tending his Antique Shop in North London which is called Out Of Time, the title of his 1966 hit which was the No. 1 song when Englands won the World Cup.

FENTON, Shane and the FENTONES

See STARDUST, Alvin.

Chris Farlowe and his antique shop (right)

FELICIANO, Jose

Guitarist and jazz singer who crossed over into pop in the late 1960s. He opened his own recording studio in 1972 before concentrating on releasing work in his native Spanish for which he won three Grammy awards. *Light My Fire (1968).*

Julie Felix

FELIX, Julie

Continues to be an active campaigner for womens rights, environmental issues and at one time founded Britain's first New Age folk club.

FERRY, Bryan

See ROXY MUSIC.

FIFTH DIMENSION

Despite Gold Discs on both sides of the

Celebrity Loves

Ten who keep it glamourous

1 Jackson Browne:
   Daryl Hannah *Actress*
2 Thomas Dolby:
   Kathleen Beller *Actress, Kathy Colby in Dynasty*
3 Phil May (Pretty Things):
   Married into aristocracy and attended Charles & Di's wedding
4 Jean Michelle Jarre
   Charlotte Rampling *Actress*
5 Ringo Starr:
   Barbara Bach *Bond girl*
6 Barry Ryan:
   Princess Meria of Johore
7 Brian May (Queen):
   Anita Dobson *Eastenders Actress*
8 James Taylor:
   Carly Simon *You're So Vain*
9 Phil Lynott:
   Liz Crowther *Leslie Crowther's actress daughter*
10 Anthony Newley:
   Joan Collins *Actress/novelist and uncrowned queen celebrity love*

Atlantic and a large international following, the group's recording career went into decline in the mid-Seventies. A reunion in 1975 failed miserably. Marilyn McCoo and Billy Davis Junior reappeared eighteen months later with You Don't Have To Be A Star and they have continued to work together ever since. Lead singer McCoo also has pursued a career on television, presenting the show Solid Gold and appearing in the soap series Days Of Our Lives.

FITZGERALD, Ella

Leading jazz singer Fitzgerald died in 1996.

FIVE STAR

At the peak of their success the Pearson family moved to a mansion in Sunningdale complete with home recording studio. However, their stay lasted less than three years when financial worries forced them to leave apparently only days before the bailiff

Five Star

was due in. In 1990 Stefan Pearson was convicted of committing an act of public indecency and fined £100 after an incident in a public lavatory in New Malden, Surrey. In the Nineties a gold and silver disc were auctioned for a mere £1,500. Their next album was made available for licensing on the groups own Tent label in March 1994.

FLACK, Roberta

Atlantic soul singer Flack broke into the international big time when the Clint Eastwood film Play Misty For Me featured her song The First Time Ever I saw Your Face in 1972. In addition to several solo hits, she struck up a successful partnership with Donny Hathaway which kept her in the pop charts well into the late Seventies (Hathaway died in 1979). Despite relatively little chart activity since she has continued to successfully tour the world for the past three decades. *Killing Me Softly With His Song (1973).*

FLEETWOOD MAC

In 1969 Albatross was at the top of the British charts, however, group leader Peter Green left within a year and was closely followed by guitarist Jeremy Spencer and then Danny Kirwan. The band then endured many

changes but re-emerged in the mid-Seventies for a ten year span back at the top with the album Rumours selling more than 15 million copies. Kirwan recorded a solo album for DJM before being admitted to a psychiatric hospital. Jeremy Spencer joined a religious cult (The Children Of God) in Italy. Bob

Brunning became a schoolteacher and is now a headmaster. In 1977 Peter Green was committed to a mental hospital and then worked as a grave digger and hospital porter before returning to record and perform live as The Peter Green Splinter Group which features Neil Murray and Cozy Powell. In 1994 Mick Fleetwood opened his own eatery and blues club in Alexandria called Fleetwoods

Eddie Floyd

Fleetwood Mac

Restaurant, while Lindsey Buckingham and Stevie Nicks teamed up for the single Twister, the title song from the film of the same name.

FLINT, Berni
Opportunity Knocks winner still lives in Southport and is busier now than he has ever been. Working for a large part of the year with Jim Davidson in Summer season he also does live concerts and Christmas panto.
I Don't Want To Put A Hold On You (1977).

FLOWERPOT MEN
see WHITE PLAINS.

FLOYD, Eddie
Currently lives in Italy and is still performing. His hobby is collecting versions of his biggest hit, Knock on Wood, which has been covered by a multitude of stars including David Bowie, Cher, Eric Clapton, and Amii Stewart who reached the top ten in England twice with the song (1979 and 1985).

FONTANA, Wayne & Mindbenders
Born Glynn Ellis, Wayne (took his stage name from the Fontana Records label) and his skiffle backing group had a top ten hit on both sides of the Atlantic with Game Of Love – six months later they had broken up. Former Mindbenders Eric Stewart and Graham Gouldman later formed Hotlegs (Neanderthal Man, 1970) and then 10cc. Bob Lang dropped out of music but re-emerged as a member of Racing Cars in 1976 (They Shoot Horses Dont They) then quit again to run a stereo equipment company. Ric Rothwell has gone on to set up his own antiques business. In 1970 Fontana gave up singing to work for Chappell Music Publishers as resident songwriter before resuming a recording career in 1976. However the mainstay of his current work is on the cabaret circuit. A Groovy Kind of Love also topped the English charts many years later for Phil Collins.

FORD, Emile
Of West Indian origin, Emile Ford sprung to prominence in 1959 with the multi million seller What Do You Want To Make Those Eyes At Me For? Now lives in a terraced house in Liverpool and still plays live in small clubs around the country.

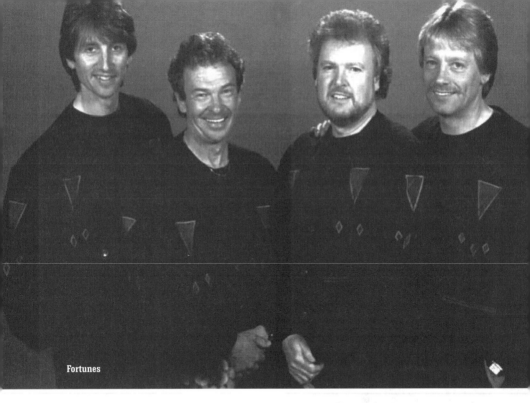

Fortunes

FORMBY, George

Banjo playing comedian from Wigan excelled long before the creation of the pop charts, however he did scrape into the top forty in 1960 with Happy Go Lucky Me. He died the following year from a heart attack, but his vocals were used to help Two In A Tent to No. 25 in 1994 with their version of his best known song.
When I'm Cleaning Windows.

FORTUNES

In 1965 You've Got Your Troubles reached No. 2 in England but the following year their manager was shot dead by a business rival. After a number of years chart absence the group re-emerge with Freedom Come, Freedom Go in 1971. Founder Rod Allen lives in Birmingham and is still performing. Barry Pritchard stepped down in 1995 due to ill health and runs a bar in Spain. Glen Dale left in the Sixties but still plays in Leicester. Chris Capaldi (brother of Jim) lives in Cheltenham and plays the blues at local venues. Andy Brown runs a post office in Worcester.
Storm In A Teacup (1972).

FOUNDATIONS

Formed in 1966 by eight young men who met regularly in a London coffee bar whose Baby

Clem Curtis of The Foundations

Now That I've Found You gave them a No. 1 hit and a million seller. This was followed up with the Mike D'Abo song Build Me Up Buttercup. 1968 saw the bands' fortunes begin to fade and they finally split in 1970. Singer Clem Curtis is still in regular demand with his new Foundations.

FOUR TOPS

Motown stalwarts Four Tops are still performing and had not had a personnel change in 43 years unitl the death of Lawrence Payton in July 1997.
Reach Out And I'll Be There (1966).

72

Fourmost

FOURMOST

Hello Little Girl, a top ten hit in 1963 was followed by A Little Loving the next year. In 1965 Mike Millward was admitted to hospital in Cheshire suffering from leukaemia and died in 1966 aged only 23. In 1967 the group moved into musical/comedy cabaret before eventually disbanding. The remaining members re-formed to become a strong draw in cabaret.

FOX, Samantha

Leapt from Page Three of the Sun to score three top ten entries in 1986/7. She has now released her fifth album (21st Century Fox) to maintain a singing career alongside her continuing success as a model.

FRAMPTON, Peter

After five albums with Humble Pie Frampton went solo in 1971.He spent the next five years writing and touring, culminating in Frampton Comes Alive which became the biggest selling live album ever (released in 1976 and selling 15 million copies). In 1987 he played guitar on David Bowie's Glass Spider World Tour. After a period of relative low profile playing small clubs he released Frampton Comes Alive II in 1995 and has returned to playing in front of full houses at major venues around the world.

FRANCIS, Connie

Connie Francis reached the pinnacle of her popularity when she was still in her teens but still had plenty to write about in her autobiography published in 1984 called Who's Sorry Now? In 1964 she fled a Mexico City hotel in her night dress in the midst of an earthquake, the nightclub manager pursued her with threats of legal action if she didn't return to complete her contract! Ten years later she was raped at knifepoint in her New York hotel room and she later sued the hotels owners for negligence and was awarded $3million in damages. She then became a recluse and underwent two- and-a-half years of psychiatric treatment. In 1978 she recovered from nasal surgery which went wrong and her brother George was killed in a gangland-style killing three years later. She then spent time in a rest home before returning to live in Hollywood and Las Vegas.

Frankie Goes to Hollywood

FRANKIE GOES TO HOLLYWOOD

In 1984 Relax topped the singles chart followed by Two Tribes and Power of Love, making them the first band since Gerry and the Pacemakers to have three consecutive No.1 singles. The final tour took place in 1987 with the band breaking up shortly afterwards and singer Holly Johnson going solo, as did Rutherford. In 1990 Brian Masher Marsh sold his north London home and returned to work as an electrician. Peter Jed Gill is now working for the Love Station production company, while Mark OToole moved to Los Angeles to work on some demos but returned to Liverpool in 1992. Johnson, who revealed that he is HIV positive, still performs.

FRANKLIN, Aretha

Aretha Franklin continues to stamp her authority as one of soul music's foremost exponents forty years on from her first album, The Gospel Sound Of Aretha Franklin, recorded in church. In addition to the gold and platinum albums; 15 Grammies; Honorary Doctorate in Law; her voice has been proclaimed one of Michigan's natural resources!

A Free montage from 1973
and a memorial plaque to
Paul Kossoff (below)

PAUL KOSSOFF
1950-1976 All right now

FRED John and the PLAYBOY BAND

One hit wonder John Fred has since carved a career as a producer.

Judy In Disguise (With Glasses) (1968).

FREDDIE & The Dreamers

Freddy Garrity was nicknamed The Clown Prince of Pop and scored bubble-gum hits with If You Gotta Make A Fool Of Somebody and I'm Telling You Now. After a television series The Little Big Time he returned to British cabaret clubs with a new set of Dreamers. The original members have now all left the music business. Derek Quinn who was lead guitarist is working for a soft drinks company; Pete Birrell, the bass player, is now a taxi driver; Ray Crewston, rhythm guitarist, runs a bar in the Canary Islands.

FREE

Named by Alexis Korner, the band split in 1971 after a decline following the success of Alright Now. They briefly reformed in 1972 but Simon Kirke then left and recently toured the USA with Ringo Starr's All Stars. Paul Rodgers formed Bad Company, making the top twenty with Can't Get Enough. Guitarist Andy Fraser went on to work with Brain Eno and Robert Palmer and is now based in Los Angeles working occasionally as a songwriter and producer. Kossoff, the son of famous actor David, died in 1976 whilst on an aeroplane – the cause of death was heart failure due to drug abuse. Rodgers, now successfully recording and touring alone, admits 'women, booze, drugs – you name it, we did it all' and he is thankful to have survived it all. Now aged 47, he is the father of two sons aged 24 and 20 who have their own group, The Boa Band.
Alright Now (1970 & 1991).)

FREY, Glenn

See THE EAGLES.

FRIEDMAN, Dean

American singer who scored three successive hits in 1978 and then promptly vanished from the public eye. After almost 10 years re-emerged as soundtrack composer and performer on I Bought A Vampire Motorcycle, horror film. His female partner was Denise Marsa.
Lucky Stars (1978).

FURY, Billy

In 1967 the former Sixties teen idol was diagnosed as having heart problems. He then spent much of his time on his farm breeding horse and pursuing animal conservation interests. In 1973 he starred in the film That'll Be The Day and in 1981, after 11 years of retirement, renewed his recording career with Polydor Records but died from heart failure less than three years later. A lectern inscribed in his honour was consecrated at Liverpool Cathedral in 1993, and a garden bench near his grave at Mill Hill cemetery serves as a memorial to him.

Drink!

Ten with booze-related deaths

1 Bon Scott (AC/DC)
2 Billie Holliday
3 John Bonham (Led Zeppelin)
4 Ruby Murray
5 Brian Jones (Rolling Stones)
6 Clyde McPhatter (Drifters)
7 David Byron (Uriah Heep)
8 Gene Vincent
9 Keith Moon (Who)
10 Florence Ballard (Supremes)

FULLER, Bobby Four

Was found dead in his car outside his Hollywood home in 1966 provoking suspicion that he had been killed by mobsters. He had the original hit of I Fought The Law But The Law Won in 1966 which was later covered by the Clash more than twenty years later.

Billy Fury
(behind)

GALLAGHER, Rory

A legendary Irish guitarist whose Live In Europe album achieved a top ten chart placing in 1972. Gallagher died in June 1995 due to complications following a liver transplant.

GALLAGHER and LYLE

Previously members of McGuinness Flint who had a hit When I'm Dead and Gone, then had hits as a duo with: Break Away, I Want to Stay with You, and My Heart on My Sleeve. They parted in 1979, Gallagher moving to film and TV films and Lyle becoming a full-time songwriter. He wrote hits for Tina Turner such as What's Love Got to Do With It? and We Dont Need Another Hero. Re-formed in 1988 and have continued to perform together occasionally ever since.

GARRETT, Leif

Teenage heart-throb who had a brief brush with fame during the 1979 craze for skateboards. Released I Was Made For Dancing before resuming an acting career which has since included a small part alongside Tom Cruise in The Outsider.

GAYE, Marvin

Despite being one of Motown's biggest stars with a string of huge hits to his name, Gaye had a deeply troubled life and filed for bankruptcy in 1978. Six years later, suffering from cocaine addiction, he announced to his family that he was going to commit suicide. His life came to a sad end when in April of the same year he was shot dead by his father during a violent argument. His father was later sentenced to five years for voluntary manslaughter.

I Heard it Through the Grapevine (1969).

Gazza

Marvin Gaye

GAZZA

Flawed football genius Paul Gascoigne helped fellow Geordies Lindisfarne to return to the charts after a twelve year absence.

Fog On The Tyne (revisited) (1990).

GENESIS

Mike Rutherford (guitar) and Tony Banks (keyboards) are the only Genesis members to remain from the 1967 version who sent a demo tape to Jonathan King. Peter Gabriel was the lead singer before launching a solo career and drummer Phil Collins filled the breach at the same time as developing a one-band music industry. In 1997 Collins decided to concentrate on his solo recording and acting career and the relatively unknown 28 year old Ray Wilson took his place in the supergroup. In 1996 Rutherford and Banks invested in Cambridge Technology Display, a company producing leading-edge lighting the band are interested in using for their spectacular stage shows.

GENTRY, Bobby

During the Seventies had her own British television series and won two Gold records and three Grammy Awards. However she had to rely on the film version of her Ode To Billy Joe, which told the story of Billy Joe Macallister's suicide from Tallahatchie Bridge to revive her somewhat flagging fortunes. This has allowed her to step back into the limelight of Las Vegas and Reno nightclubs.

I'll Never Fall In Love Again (1969).

Gerry & The Pacemakers

GERRY & The Pacemakers

Synonymous with Merseybeat; Liverpool Football Club and the Ferry that crosses the river Mersey Gerry Marsden and his Pacemakers became members of the select band of musicians (now including the Spice Girls!) who can boast three consecutive number ones with their first three releases. After a spell acting on stage and presenting a children's television show, Gerry re-formed the Pacemakers in 1975, then again in 1979. They still travel the club circuit and the band name has become established in another field – Gerry's brother Fred (drums) now teaches people how to drive through his Pacemaker Driving School.

You'll Never Walk Alone (1963).

GIBB, Andy

Topped the American charts with his first three singles and enjoyed a well-publicised relationship with Dallas TV star Victoria Principal. He became addicted to cocaine, filed for bankruptcy in 1988, and later in the same year died of heart failure, just after his 30th birthday.

GILLAN

Heavy metal band formed by Deep Purple vocalist Ian Gillan. Drummer Mick Underwood has just recorded an album with Nick Simper (first Deep Purple guitarist) called Quartermass 2. John McCoy and Bernie Torme have worked on various projects including their own solo works. Colin Towns has produced a number of musical scores including music for the BBC TV series Pie In The Sky.

GILTRAP, Gordon

His biggest commercial hit, Heartsong, was the theme to BBC TVs Holiday Programme for seven years. The guitar has been his career (having released 25 albums to date) and he owns a guitar shop in Knowle, Warwickshire, as well as being a classical composer. He made a stage appearance as Troubadour in Cliff Richard's Heathcliff.

Gordon Giltrap

GLITTER, Gary

It is now 25 years since mild mannered Paul Gadd was transformed into The King of Glam Rock. In 1976 after a succession of hits he decided to retire from showbusiness for personal reasons. The Inland Revenue and a London Bankruptcy court can be thanked for the return to showbusiness for one of Britains most entertaining performers. The need to clear debts prompted live dates and one of the most unusual auctions to take place at Sothebys – a sale of some of his bizarre and extravagant stage costumes. Having beaten the bankruptcy of the Eighties he continues to perform his famous Gang Show to a new following, particularly each Christmas. Producer and arranger on most of hits, Mike Leander, (who had previously worked with The Beatles and the Drifters) died of cancer in 1996 at the age of 54.

I'm The Leader Of The Gang (I Am) (1973).

Gary Glitter now

Glitter Band

GLITTER BAND

Created in 1972 to provide backing for Gary Glitter and went on to have considerable success in their own right. Gerry Shepherd and Pete Phipps were the founder members of the band and Gerry's star shaped guitar and Pete's familiar drum beat still create the distinctive glam rock sound

Gary Glitter in 1972

today. Founder member and main singer John Springate now owns and runs his own recording studio.

GODLEY & CREME

See 10cc.

GOLDSBORO, Bobby

A Seventies sentamentalist with Honey being the song that made him into a star. In 1973 he charted once more with Summer (The First Time) followed by Hello Summertime – subsequently used as a film and TV advert soundtrack for Coca Cola. He is still involved in songwriting, producing and recording and still makes live appearances on the cabaret circuit in America.

GOODIES

Comic trio who extended the success of their popular television series (which earned them all an OBE) into the pop charts with all time classics like Funky Gibbon and Black Pudding Bertha!

78

Doctor Graeme Garden has now utilised his previous training to produce a series of humorous videos with to help patients with their medical complaints. Bill Oddie is now better known as an ornithologist and presenter of nature programmes. Tim Brooke Taylor is a regular on radio.

GOONS

The Ying Tong Song provided The Goons with a top three spot in 1956 and again managed to break into the top ten when released seventeen years later. Harry Secombe was knighted in 1981, suffered from peritonitis, slimmed down and presented the religious programme Highway. Peter Sellers, who died in 1980, had established himself as a screen actor as Inspector Clouseau in the Pink Panther films and almost won an Oscar for his last film – Being There. Spike Milligan still puts in the occasional manic appearance on screen and stage, in between time he fights for ecological causes from his north London home.

GORE, Lesley

Enjoyed two big hits on both sides of the Atlantic in the early Sixties with It's My Party which topped the US charts and Judy's Turn To Cry. Having faded from view she studied for a Bachelor Of Arts degree then burst back onto the music scene by penning lyrics for the 1980 movie Fame, directed by Alan Parker. Most of the music for the film was composed by her brother Michael. She still bangs out the old favourites on the nostalgia circuit in America and a revival of her hit You Don't Own Me featured in the film First Wives Club. *It's My Party (1963).*

GRAND FUNK RAILROAD

Formed in Michigan in 1968, Grand Funk Railroad recorded seven albums and their Were An American Band reached No. 1 in the US singles chart before the band finally split in 1977. A crisis had been overcome in 1972 when they sacked their manager, Terry Knight, who responded by seizing all their equipment. Mark Farmer (singer) followed a solo path while Craig Frost (keyboards) joined Bob Seger's Silver Bullet Band. Mel Schacher (bass) took to restoring old Jaguar motor cars, although he did attempt to reform the band in 1981 but this did not materialise because

Motor Death

Ten who perished in road accidents

1. Alan Barton (Smokie) *1995*
2. Marc Bolan *1977* & Steve Curry *1981* (Both T-Rex)
3. Clarence White (Byrds) *Killed by drunk driver*
4. Harry Chapin *1981 – Car Exploded into flames*
5. Eddie Cochran *1960 – Crashed on A4 during British tour*
6. Johnny Horton *1960– In Texas*
7. London Boys *1996 – Both died together in the Alps*
8. Jerry Edmonton *1993* Rushton Morebe *1981* (Both from Steppenwolf)
9. Dickie Valentine *1971*
10. Johnny Kidd *1966*

Farmer wanted to concentrate on the Health Food Shop he had since opened.

GRANT, David

See LINX.

GRANT, Eddy

Formerly a member of The Equals, who he left in 1972 to become a producer and to set up his own record label Ice Records. Enjoyed a batch of solo hits in the late Seventies and early Eighties before returning to live in Barbados and concentrate on his business interests. Attracted press attention when he controversially tried to outbid Bob Marley's family for the rights to the Jamaican's songs.

GRAY, Dobie

Drift Away gave Dobie Gray his first American No. 1 but remarkably it failed to make any impact in England until a version by Michael Bolton charted in 1992. Gray tried his hand at acting, but now records and performs as a country artist.

GREEN, Al

Eight time grammy award winner, the original Soul Man has now become the Minister Of Soul having been ordained as the Pastor of the Full Gospel Tabernacle Church in

Memphis in 1976. The Right Reverend Green has now been providing his own brand of gospel and R&B for three decades and also managed a stint in the Broadway Musical Your Arms Are Too Short To Box With God. While continuing with his ministry, Al still tours world-wide.

GREENBAUM, Norman

A one-hit wonder with Spirit In The Sky which topped the UK charts in 1970. Having retired from music to run a dairy farm in Petaluma, California his finances were given a lift when Doctor And The Medics topped the chart with the same song in 1986.

Nick Heywood of Haircut 100 now

HAIRCUT 100

Had four consecutive top ten hits in 1981/82 fronted by fresh faced teen idol Nick Heyward. In November 1982 he quit the band to become a solo artist. Now 15 years on after brief solo success he has recently signed to Creation Records with a new contract and a new single. Backing musicians Les Nemes and Phil Smith went on to perform with Rick Astley. Blair Cunningham, the group's drummer, returned to session work then joined The Pretenders before becoming a regular member of Paul McCartney's backing band in the early Nineties. Mark Fox joined East-West record label in London and signed Jimmy Nail during his spell on A & R. He is now A & R Director (International) at EMI.

HALEY, Bill & The Comets

Rock Around The Clock is periodically re-released all over the world and has sold in excess of 20,000,000 copies! Since the decline of rock and roll Haley had lived a quiet life in the Rio Grande Valley breaking out only occasionally to tour the world. In 1980 he suffered from a mystery illness which restricted him to home and died on February 9th 1981 in a Los Angeles hospital with reports circulating of a suspected brain tumour. His backing band, The Comets, continue to perform live.

HAMMER, M C

Enjoyed huge hits in the early Nineties with The Adams group and The Adams Family movie and even had his own cartoon show, The Hammer Man. In 1996 he was declared bankrupt with debts in excess of $10 million and is now working as a telephone salesman in an attempt to pay back his creditors having earned a reported $33 million in 1990 and 1991. Building a dream home in 12 acres, containing among other things two bowling alleys, paying for a 70-man entourage and Las Vegas gambling blew the fortune away. *U Can't Touch This (1990).*

HAMMOND, Albert

Before becoming a successful solo artist he had written Little Arrows – a hit for Leapy

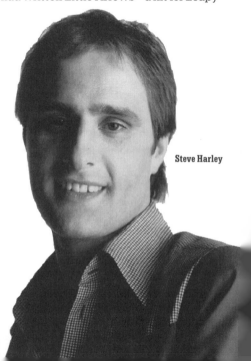

Steve Harley

Lee in 1966 – and Gimme Dat Ding which reached No. 9 in 1970 for The Pipkins. As a solo artist he had hits with It Never Rains in Southern California and Free Electric Band in the Seventies before he turned back to writing hits for other artists: When I Need You for Leo Sayer; Nothing's Gonna Stop Us Now for Starship; One Moment in Time for Whitney Houston. He also then returned to his Spanish roots in the Eighties and he topped the Spanish charts a number of times.
Free Electric Band (1973).

HARDCASTLE, Paul

Had a run of little known minor hits in the Eighties and one massive triumph when Nineteen topped the charts in 1985. Now works as a writer and producer and is responsible for the theme to BBC TVs Holiday programme.

HARDIN, Tim

Writer of the classic If I Were A Carpenter – a song which was later to give Johnny Cash and his wife June Carter a gold single. Seemed to be dogged by ill-health and there were reports and rumours of drink and drugs addiction. He lived almost as a recluse in virtual obscurity until his death in December 1980 when he was found dead from a heart attack in his Los Angeles apartment.

HARLEY, Steve

See COCKNEY REBEL.

HARPO

Already a massive star on the continent, Harpo breezed into the British charts in 1976 with the catchy Movie Star. Despite having shed his mop of curly hair (replaced by a shiny scalp!), he continues to draw big crowds in his native Sweden and at nostalgia concerts in Germany.

HARRIS, Jet & Tony MEEHAN

See THE SHADOWS.

HARRIS, Rolf

Australian songster and master of the paintbrush, digeredoo and wobbling board. Sixties hits included Tie Me Kangaroo Down Sport and the 1969 No. 1 Two Little Boys. He enjoyed elevation to cult status on the college circuit when his rendition of Led Zeppelin's Stairway To Heaven provided him with a surprising return to the top ten in 1993. Now lives in a beautiful riverside home in Berkshire (unfortunately prone to flooding however) and enjoys regular television work including the role of presenting Animal Hospital.

HARRISON, Noel

Actor, singer, composer, musician, screenwriter and carpenter! After falling out with the movie establishment he fled to live in Nova Scotia in the Seventies where he designed and built his own home. Having made his peace with Hollywood he returned to live and work in Los Angeles and recently starred as Professor Higgins in My Fair Lady at the Musical Theatre, Texas – the role made famous by his father, the legendary actor, Sir Rex.

Windmills Of Your Mind from the film The Thomas Crown Affair (1969).

HARRISON, George

See The BEATLES.

HARTMAN, Dan

Retired from performing to work in production from his own Connecticut studio after massive disco smashes Instant Replay and This Is It. Briefly re-emerged in 1985 to have an American top 10 with I Can Dream from the film Streets Of Fire before returning to his mixing desk. Produced Tina Turner's Foreign Affair album which topped the charts in twelve countries. Hartman died on March 22nd 1994 at home in Bridgeport, Connecticut at the age of 43 after a prolonged battle with AIDS.

HARVEY, Alex

Rocker who died in February 1982 having suffered a major heart attack while in Belgium as part of a European Tour. Chris Glen joined MSG and undertook session work before becoming a car salesman. Zal Cleminson joined Nazareth and Elkie Brooks' backing band but is now working as a computer programmer. A brief reformation took place in the Nineties but all have now given up music with the exception of Ted McKenna who runs his own drum clinics.

Delilah (1975).

HAVENS, Richie

Black folk guitarist who appeared at both the Woodstock and Isle Of Wight festivals. Now a successful painter, sculptor and writer, he successfully boosts his income by supplying voice overs for American television commercials.

HAWKES, Chesney

Son of Tremeloes star Chip Hawkes who has been working in the USA since appearing in the musical stage show Buddy's Song with Roger Daltrey.

The One And Only (1991).

HAWKWIND

Prone to recording under the influence of LSD from their own little community in Notting Hill. Michael Moorcock, once Hawkwind's occasional narrator and lyricist, is now a cult writer of science fiction novels. In fact Dave Brock, the only original member still performing with a group, is still fascinated with sci-fi and possesses a huge library dedicated to the subject. Del Dettmar who played keyboards upped and left for Canada in the early Nineties where he can now be found playing his double pitted guitar by one of the famous great lakes.

Silver Machine (1972).

HAWKINS, Edwin, Singers

Oh Happy Day, their solitary hit, still provides credibility for the current version of the Singers. Still performing live but now with much fewer than the original fifty members who reached No. 2 in the charts in1969.

HAYES, Isaac

Academy Award winning composer, musician and actor best known for composing the Oscar winning Theme From Shaft in 1972. Years later he had to file for bankruptcy with debts of $6 million and in 1989 he was jailed for owing $346,000 in child support and alimony. Now a veteran actor, having appeared in more than twenty-five films, he has been actively involved in the Civil Rights movement since its early days and also has the distinction of being crowned a 'King' in Ghana in return for his help in introducing investors to the country.
Theme From Shaft (1971).

HAYWARD, Justin

See MOODY BLUES.

HAYSI FANTAYSEE

Jeremy Healy has been playing, writing and mixing for Boy George and appears in some of the best clubs in the country having established himself as one of the top rave mixers on the scene. Kate Garner is now pursuing a career as a professional photographer.

HEATWAVE

Anglo/American outfit who broke into British

Heatwave

charts in 1977 with disco hit Boogie Nights. The subsequent years have been a mix of musical success and personal disaster for members of the band: Guitarist Jessie Whitten was fatally stabbed in 1977; Rod Temperton, (keyboards) left in 1978 to concentrate on songwriting, for, amongst others, George Benson and Aretha Franklin – his best-known track is Thriller by Michael Jackson; in 1978 Mario Mantese (bass) was paralysed in a car accident him forcing him to leave the group; Johnny Wilder Jnr, the singer, is paralysed from the neck down in a 19790 car accident in New York but with the help of a wheelchair returns to performing; Ernest Berger left the group in 1982.Three of the original members have hung in there and are still performing under the Heatwave name.
Mind Blowing Decisions (1978).

HEAVY METAL KIDS

Enjoyed a brief but loud pop career in the Seventies before frontman Gary Holton departed to become better known as Wayne in the TV series'Auf Wiedersehen Pet. His acting career was short-lived as Holton died from a drugs overdose during filming.

HEINZ

Peroxide blond haired former bass guitarist with the Tornados, Heinz Burt hit the top ten of 1963 with Just Like Eddie, a tribute to Eddie Cochran. He has since worked as a production worker for Ford and as a taxi driver. Now 54 and living in Eastleigh, Hampshire he has been forced to retire due to ill health
Just Like Eddie (1963).

HELLO

Bob Bradbury, Keith Marshall, Vic Faulkener and Jeff Allen had a hit in the mid-

Hello

Jimi Hendrix and
memorial plaque

ENGLISH HERITAGE

JIMI
HENDRIX
1942~1970
Guitarist and
Songwriter
lived here
1968~1969

HENDRIX, Jimi

One of the stars of Woodstock and hailed as among the best electric guitarists ever. His ability to make his guitar speak combined with a gutsy singing voice elevated him from ex-paratrooper to world fame before excessive drug taking prematurely ended both his life and career but created a rock legend. He died on 18th September 1970 as a result of inhalation of vomit due to barbiturate intoxication. In 1997 a National a Heritage Blue plaque was unveiled on his former home in Brook Street, London.

Voodoo Chile (1970).

HENLEY, Don

See THE EAGLES.

HERMANS HERMITS

Led by Peter Noone the Hermits sold a phenomenal 50,000,000 records world-wide, with 20 hit singles. Peter Noone also appeared in the soap Coronation Street (in which he played Len Fairclough's son, Stanley) and left the group in 1972 to go solo and to act. He

Seventies with Tell Him, a re-make of Billie Davis' 1963 smash. They disappeared from the scene for almost 20 years after fading from the British charts although they had continued to thrive in Germany until 1979 when the band broke up. Marshall went on to a solo career achieving success with Only Crying (No.12 in 1991). Bob Bradbury has now reformed Hello with three new members and released a 13 track album of Glam Rock Classics in 1996 entitled Glam Rockers.

New York Groove (1975).

City of Westminster.
GENTLEMEN

Herman's Hermits then (main pic) and now

Imortalised

Ten whose names live on

1. **Alright Now**
   Inscription on Paul Kossoff's (Free) memorial
2. **Seasons In The Sun**
   Name of Terry Jack's yacht
3. **Sticky Fingers**
   Bill Wyman's Restaurant
4. **Argent**
   Sheet music shop in London
5. **Out Of Time**
   Antique shop
6. **Rydell High School (Grease)**
   Named after Bobby Rydell
7. **Twitty City**
   Conway Twitty's fun park
8. **Berry Park**
   Chuck Berry's version of above
9. **Imagine**
   Mosaic memorial in New York
10. **Van Zant Park**
    Named in honour of former Lynryd Skynryd singer Ronnie

a PA company, his own tilingbusiness and still plays now and again.

Frank Renshaw (lead singer between 1980-2) later wrote Glory Glory Man Utd which reached No. 13 in 1983. HE then took a job as Entertainment Director for a Yugoslavia-based hotel chain.
No Milk Today (1966).

HEYWARD, Nick

See HAIRCUT 100.

HIGGINS, Bertie

Now teaches basics of singing to Hollywood star Bert Reynolds' acting classes. Has also opened the Bertie Higgins Rum Runners Holiday Bar in Florida Quays.
Key Largo (1982).

HILL, Benny

Although remembered for his saucy seaside postcard humour, Hill was acting in comedy films from the early Sixties and reached No. 12 in the charts with his Gather In The Mushrooms as early as 1961. He suffered a heart attack in 1992 and died from a further attack on the same day as his friend and fellow comic Frankie Howerd.
Ernie (The Fastest Milkman In The West) (1971).

HOLLIDAY, Billie

Blues legend depicted by Diana Ross who starred in Lady Sings The Blues, the story of this tragic queen of the blues. Holliday died in July 1959 from cirrhosis of the liver, having been addicted to alcohol and heroin.

HOLLIES

Still performing today and have managed to maintain the phenomenal success that they originally generated in the Swinging Sixties. Founder members Allan Clarke, Tony Hicks and Bobby Elliott have now been joined by ex-Mud bass guitarist Ray Stiles in the current line-up.

Original guitarist Graham Nash had left in 1968 to become part of the legendary Crosby, Stills, Nash & Young however he was reunited with his former colleagues in 1996 when he flew in from Los Angeles to record a remarkable track for the MCA album Not Fade Away. With the help of cutting-edge recording technology a new version of Peggy Sue Got Married was created featuring the

later moved to France (home of his wife Mirelle). Noone's next stop was America where besides writing and production work, he still found time to open a clothes shop in New York called The Zoo Boutique. Although he has been based in Los Angeles, Noone has continued in cabaret and theatrical stage roles appearing in the stage musical Pirates of Penzance in 1982 in the West End. Noone now lives near Santa Barbara, California and appears as a VJ on the US Cable TV channel VH1 as well as being an interviewer for the station's music magazine.

The Hermits continue to perform on the nostalgia circuit led by original drummer and former hairdresser Barry Whitwam. The band also features former Salford Jets members Geoff Kerry and Geoff Foot. The original lead guitarist Lek Leckenby died in 1994 of Lymphoma in Manchester. Keith Hopwood (rhythm guitar) now owns his own recording studio in Cheshire where he specialises in producing jingles. Karl Green (bass) lives in Sunbury-on-Thames and keeps busy running

voice of Buddy Holly – backed by The Hollies! An even less likely liaison was formed when the group joined the cast of Coronation Street to perform He Ain't Heavy, He's My Brother as part of the TV soap's 35th anniversary celebrations.

Drummer Don Rathbone left the group to join Shane Fenton and the Fentones (see Alvin Stardust) and was replaced by former-Fentone drummer Bobby Elliott. In 1966 Eric Haydock was taken ill and left the group to run a music shop in Stockport. He returned in 1991 playing with the New Mindbenders. The following year however he changed the band's name to Eric Haydock's Hollies – much to the disgust of his former mates. It has since taken several court injunctions to result in the name Eric Haydock ex-Hollies. Founder-member Allan Clarke left briefly in 1971 to embark on a solo singing career and

Tony Hicks is heavily involved in record production and writing. Bobby Elliott, an original member still in the band, married Tony Hicks's sister in 1994.

Ray Stiles who joined in 1986 co-owns the Pelican Recording studio in London and also plays in his own band– Taboo– in which his wife Annie is the singer.
He Ain't Heavy, He's My Brother (1969 & 1980).

HOLLY, Buddy

An inspiration for whole generation of singer/songwriters. In 1959 Holly died in a plane crash along with Richie Valens and the Big Bopper. In 1980 a statue of Buddy Holly was erected in his memory at the Lubbock Civic Centre in Texas. Ten years later the West End stage show Buddy opens in his honour. In 1978 Gary Busey took the lead role in the film The Buddy Holly Story.

HOLMES, Rupert

Best remembered for Escape – more widely known as the Pina Colada song. Holmes was previously a member of The Cufflinks who had a hit with Tracy in 1969. He Turned to composing for Broadway and won five Tony Awards for his first major production The Mystery of Edwin Drood.

HONEYBUS

Memories of the Seventies television advertisment for Nimble Bread showing an attractive girl floating in a hot air balloon should prompt the humming of I Can't Let Maggie Go. Honeybus's one and only hit was performed by Peter Dello who gave up showbiz to become a music teacher living in Wembley, north London.

HONEYCOMBS

Pop band who in the Sixties had the novelty of a female drummer, Anne 'Honey' Lantree. In the late-Sixties the Honeycombs drifted into club and variety performances before breaking up. Denis D'ell, the group's singer, attempted a come-back as a solo performer during the Seventies, appearing on ITV's talent show Opportunity Knocks.

Peter Pyne reverted to signwriting while Alan Ward went into selling musical equipment. Now Anne 'Honey' Lantree's two sons have grown up she has invested in a new drum kit and The Honeycombs reunite for occasional nostalgia performances.
Have I The Right (1964).

HOPKIN, Mary

In 1968 Mary Hopkin appeared on the talent show Opportunity Knock and captured the interest of the nation as well as impressing Paul McCartney who produced her trademark song Those Were The Days which topped the charts all over the world, selling over eight million copies. Her Knock Knock Who's There? was the UK entry into the Eurovision Song Contest in 1970 and reached No. 2 in the charts. In 1976 If You Loved Me scraped into the top 40.

She married producer Tony Visconti and left showbusiness to start a family. Today, Mary Hopkin lives with her two children – she is parted from her husband – in the village of Wargrave in Berkshire and continues to write songs.

In 1981 having spent much time devoted to her family, Hopkin re-emerged with a group called Sundance and three years later she returned to the UK chart as lead vocalist with a band called Oasis, a group which included Peter Skellern on piano and Julian Lloyd-Webber on cello. In 1989 she released a come-back album on the Film Tracks' label and sang on George Martin's recording of Under Milk Wood playing Rosie, the whore – a far cry from the innocent folk child of the Sixties.
Those Were The Days (1968).

HORTON, Johnny

American male vocalist in the Fifties. Horton was killed in a car crash on November 5th, 1960 close to Milano, Texas.

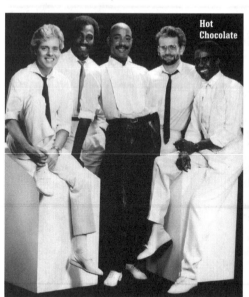
Hot Chocolate

HOT CHOCOLATE

The only British group to have a hit every year throughout the Seventies have now been touring extensively for 25 years. They even performed at Charles & Di's wedding party. When singer Errol Brown decided to leave to start a solo career, the search for his replacement was called off when Londoner Greg Bannis was spotted imitating the bald headed frontman on the television talent show Stars In Their Eyes – he has been with the band ever since. They have been given a new lease of life when their hit You Sexy Thing featuredin the film The Full Monty. The song has returned to the top 10 and put their Greatest Hits album back in the charts.
So You Win Again (1977).

HOTLEGS

See 10cc.

HOUSEMARTINS

Best known for their hit Caravan of Love which reached No. 1 in 1986. Vocalist Ted Key left the Housemartins in 1985 to open a vegetarian restaurant in Hull and in 1989 Paul Heaton, vocalist and guitarist, departed to set up Beautiful South.

Norman Cook became successful as a dance

Human League

record re-mixer, formed Beats International and topped the charts with 'Dub Be Good to Me' in 1990.

The band's original drummer, Hugh Whittaker, was remanded in custody for allegedly assaulting somebody with an axe and setting fire to his house on three occasions. He was sentenced to six years in prison.

HUDSON-FORD

See THE STRAWBS.

HUMAN LEAGUE

Now enjoying a comeback, the trio from Sheffield are fronted by former hospital porter Phillip Oakey and held the coveted number one spot during the Christmas of 1981 with Don't You Want Me? Martin Ware and Ian Craig-Marsh left the group in 1980 to form Heaven 17. The League now – Philip Oakey, Joanne Catherall and Susan Ann Sulley – are recording for East-West Records after a long term association with Virgin.

HUMBLE PIE

In 1969 their only chart entry, Natural Born Bugie, reached No. 4 in the UK. Pete Frampton (guitar and vocals) quit in 1971 to pursue a successful solo career and the group fragmented in 1975. Steve Marriott (guitar

and vocals.) formed Steve Marriott's All-Stars and then later joined a re-united Small Faces. In 1991 Marriott died in a fire at his 16th century cottage in Arkesden, Essex. Greg Ridley (bass) also joined Marriott's All Stars. Jerry Shirley (drums) later formed Natural Gas.

HUMPERDINCK, Engelbert

Born Arnold Dorsey, Engelbert can boast average sales of 5 million records per annum over a 27 year span since adopting the name of a 19th Century German composer. He now has homes in London and Los Angeles, the latter being on the site of Jayne Mansfield's legendary Pink Palace complete with heart shaped swimming pool. It is claimed that his fan club is one of the largest in the world with a reported 8 million members.

HYLAND, Brian

His songs were produced by his pal Del Shannon but he stopped recording in the late Eighties. Brian Hyland had his first hit at the age of 16 and two years later in 1962 Sealed with a Kiss was a big hit on both sides of the Atlantic. He re-emerged in the Seventies but has spent much of the past twenty years performing on the nostalgia circuit.
Itsy Bitsy Teeny Weeny Polka Dot Bikini (1960).

Frank Ifield

ICICLE WORKS

Formed in Liverpool in 1981 and gained national recognition with their single Love is a Wonderful Colour. Founder members Chris Sharrack and Chris Layne left in 1986 to be replaced by Roy Corkhill from Black and Ringo Starr's son Zak Starkey. They broke up in 1989 and Sharrack joined The La's'and World Party.

Ian McNabb, the original lead singer and driving force, is now performing solo with his backing band The Afterlife – five years ago he was broke and decided to take out a loan and record a solo album in Los Angeles with the help of by Neil Young's backing band Crazy Horse. He has also jammed with World Party who have been joined by drummer Chris Sharrock.

IFIELD, Frank

In January 1963 enjoyed No 1 hits in the British charts with consecutive single releases I Remember You, Lovesick Blues and The Wayward Wind. His roots are in country music and in 1981 starred at the International Festival of Country Music at Wembley.

Although he still performs on the cabaret circuit in the UK Frank Ifield now lives on the outskirts of Sydney.

IMAGINATION

Founder member Lee John still fronts the band but has also presented his own television show, Lee's Place. He hosted the World Disco Dance Championship and appeared in the cult TV show Doctor Who. *Body Talk (1981)*.

IMPRESSIONS

Originally featured Curtis Mayfield on vocals and achieved their biggest success with an American No. 4 in 1963 called It's Alright. Eleven years later First Impression became the group's only UK chart entry reaching No. 16. Mayfield had quit in 1970 to start his solo career while a version of the band has continued to perform in the States to date.

ISLEY BROTHERS

Best known in Britain for Summer Breeze and Harvest For The World in the mid Seventies but with a long Motown pedigree behind them from the early Sixties when they recorded the classic Twist and Shout which sold a million, and was later recorded by numerous other groups, including The Beatles.

Vernon Isley was killed in a car accident before the group's greatest successes and back in 1963 they briefly added an unknown guitarist – Jimi Hendrix – to the line up. O'Kelly Isley died from a heart attack in 1985 leaving only Ronald and Rudolph to hold the torch . Rudolph has also recently released a solo gospel album called houting For Jesus. *This Old Heart Of Mine (1968).*

JACKS, Terry

Terry Jacks had a worldwide No. 1 in 1974 which made him enough money to retire to a waterside retreat in Canada and to buy himself an ocean going yacht which he named after his smash Seasons in the Sun.

He now spends his time as an environmental activist and award winning video producer. He made a return to the stage in Norway but lost a stone beforehand to avoid been seen as a 'fat ageing rock star'.

JACKSON, Jermaine
see THE JACKSON FIVE.

JACKSON, Joe

Now on different path from the early music that brought him to prominence and working in the area between rock and classical music. Best known for his 1979 hit Is She Really Going out With Him? and the 1980 It's Different for Girls. A period of illness in 1981 prompted change of direction and his music reflected blues and jazz influences coupled with a move to New York. In 1994 he wrote the music for a children's video story book – The White Cat – and ventured into the world of film scores. In 1996 decided not to renew his contract with Virgin to produce himself and a double CD compilation released in 1997. A modern ballet performed to his music was a hit at the American Dance Festival in 1997.

JACKSON 5/The Jacksons/ The Jackson Family

Jackie, Randy, Tito, Jermaine, Marlon and Michael. In the Seventies and Eighties they could do no wrong and enjoyed more than 25 hits including the 1977 No. 1 Show You The Way To Go. Since those heady days of family togtherness however Michael has not been alone in the headlines!

In 1980 Randy was seriously injured in a car crash and nearly died in hospital when a nurse injected him by accident with methadone. In 1991 he was sentenced to one month in jail for beating his wife and the following year is committed to a psychiatric ward for further treatment.

In 1986 Jackie was divorced amid accusations of physical attacks and banned from visiting his home by a Judge.

In 1980 Jermaine has a top ten hit with Let's Get Serious and ten years later produced a TV show called The Jacksons: An American Dream about the family's life

In 1994 Marlon launches his own solo career and two years later Tito's three sons, all called Tito and known as 3T, reached No. 2 in England with their single Anything. His ex-wife drowned in a swimming pool accident in 1994.

Michael proposes to open a $100 million

TV & Film

Ten with no end to their talents

1 Jilted John
   Now John Shuttlworth on TV
2 Clare Grogan
   Gregorys Girl 2 in production
3 Mike Berry
   Appeared in Worzel Gummidge
4 Bobby Crush
   An unlikely Frank N Furter in The Rocky Horror Show
5 Aled Jones
   Graduated form drama school
6 Adam Ant
   Appeared in The Equaliser
7 Kemp Brothers (Spandau Ballet)
   The Krays
8 Chesney Hawkes & Roger Daltrey
   Buddy's Song
9 Sheena Easton
   Seen in Miami Vice
10 Noddy Holder (Slade)
   One of The Grimleys

The Jam

amusement park a la Disney near Warsaw in Poland.

Their sister LaToya claimed child abuse in her book Growing Up In The Jackson Family and made two appearances in Playboy magazine.

JAM

Formed in 1976 by three Woking lads, Paul Weller (vocals), Rick Buckler (guitar) and Bruce Foxton (bass). They hit the top twenty in England with 20 single releases, including four number ones: Going Underground, Start, A Town Called Malice and Beat Surrender. When the group split in 1982 Weller continued making music in the form of The Style Council, despite having being sued by the other two for an alleged £200,000 which they claimed they were owed for back royalties. Foxton joined a re-formed Stiff Little Fingers while Buckler joined Time UK before leaving music to set up a manufacturing business in West Byfleet where he makes upholstery for kit car maker Panther Cars.

Paul Weller

JAMES, Rick

In 1985 Rick James arranged and produced Eddie Murphy's big debut album which reached No. 2 in US album charts. Six years later in 1991 James and his girlfriend were arrested at his Hollywood home and charged with assault with a deadly weapon, false imprisonment and then released on $1million bail. In 1994 James was sentenced to five years' imprisonment for cocaine use and assaulting two women and was eleased from California's Folsom State prison having served just over 2 years of a five year sentence.

JAMES, Tommy & The Shondells

James formed Shondells at the age of 12 and achieved 23 gold discs and sold over 100 million records in their heyday. A Shondells

album cover in 1966 was the first professional shoot for Linda Eastman (McCartney). Having recovered from a near fatal collapse caused by drug abuse in 1973 he returned to performing live on the club circuit. Billy Idol covered his Mony Mony and Tiffany covered I Think We're Alone Now, the first reaching No.1 in America and the second No. 1 in the UK. James continues to write and record his own songs.

Mony Mony (1968).

JAN & DEAN

Jan Berry and Dean Torrence went to high school together in Los Angeles. Dean sang lead on the Beach Boys' Barbara Ann and Brian Wilson often worked on Jan and Dean recordings.

Jan was involved in a serious car smash and totally paralysed for over a year. After a lengthy spell out of the business the duo are now celebrating 30 years of live appearances and are back performing. Dean – a qualified doctor – also ran a Hollywood studio, designing posters and LP covers.

JANUS, Samantha

Now instantly recognisable on television starring in Game On and Pie in the Sky. Janus spent three weeks in the singles chart in 1991 with A Message to Your Heart, the British Eurovision Song Contest entry for that year

JAPAN

South London glam band formed in 1977 by brothers David Sylvian and Steve Jansen, with Richard Barbieri and Mick Karn. The band split up in 1982. Vocalist Sylvian continued as a solo artist and working with a variety of partners including Riuchi Sakamoto and Robert Fripp. He also had an exhibition at the Hamilton Gallery in London, displaying his photo montages. In 1989 the band briefly reformed as Japan and in 1991 again re-united this time under the name of Rain Tree Crow. They appeared in concert in 1997 under the name Jansen/Barbieri/Karn.

JETHRO TULL

Ian Anderson still dusts off his trusty flute to perform some thirty years on from the band's original formation. Having worked as a toilet cleaner in London in the early days, he now lives in splendour on the Isle of Skye where

Jethro Tull

his salmon processing plant is one of the most successful in the country.
Living In The Past (1969).

JETT, Joan & The Blackhearts

Former member of the Runaways who hit the charts with I Love Rock n Roll in 1982. Back in Los Angeles after a short period in London working with ex-Sex Pistols Paul Cook and Steve Jones they are still touring extensively and after a long period without a major record deal are now signed to Warner Brothers. Jett has her own label – Blackheart Records – as an outlet for other artists.

JILTED JOHN

Graham Fellows adopted the monicker Jilted John for the single of the same name in 1978. He returned to acting and appearing in Coronation Street he more recently created and starred as the character John Shuttleworth in his ownTV and radio shows.

JIVE BUNNY

The Music Factory run by John Pickles and his son Andy created Jive Bunny who reached No. 1 with three consecutive singles. The Pickles and their Rotherham based Music Factory Entertainment Group have continued to grow ever since and now consist of six recording studios and many dance record labels as well as Pure Energy, Europe's biggest supplier of music for aerobics.

JOHN, Elton

Reg Dwight, one time keyboard player with Long John Baldry (whose christian name was adopted as part of the stage name that we all now recognise) has come a long way from his humble origins to become one of the world's most famous musicians.

JOHNSON, Holly

See FRANKIE GOES TO HOLLYWOOD.

JON & VANGELIS

See YES.

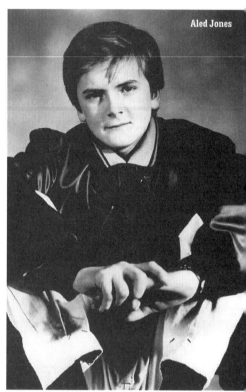

Aled Jones

JONES, Aled

The angelic voice behind Walking In The Air is now somewhat gruffer and the innocent schoolboy is now a 26 year old actor having graduated from the Bristol Old Vic theatre school in 1994.

JONES, Howard

Ten years after his last hit, Jones embarked a series of acoustic tours leaving behind the electronic gadgetry hat had become his trade mark. Jones had been dropped by label WEA in 1992 and his 1994 release Working In The Backroom was recorded at home and sold at his live shows – 20,000 copies in all. After a two year sabbatical Jones returned to live performances and in 1996 he put together a live album – Live Acoustic America – and caused a 1000 people queue in a Salt Lake City record shop in 1996 and sold the entire stock of 800 CD's in under an hour. As befits a technology freak, Jones has a website – The Howard Jones Information Network – which is operated by his parents.

JONES, Paul
See MANFRED MANN.

JONES, Tom
Knickers being thrown to him on stage, a massive income and a millionaire's lifestyle have been the norm for the boy from Wales since 1966 when The Green Green Grass of Home brought him world-wide fame. Singles like Delilah, then fifteen years later the remarkably contemporary version of Prince's Kiss have ensured that the old hip swiveller has remained in the public eye ever since.

Janis Joplin

Howard Jones

JOPLIN, Janis
Both the Leonard Cohen song Chelsea Hotel and Bette Midler's film The Rose were written about Joplin. On October 4th she was found dead at a hotel in Hollywood with fresh needle marks in her arm, her death due to accidental heroin overdose.

JUDGE DREAD
Former bouncer who managed to sell millions of records in the Seventies despite almost all of his releases being banned due to their bawdy lyrics. Big Seven and his saucy rendition of J'T'aime both breached the top ten while Y Viva Suspenders and Up With The Cock left nothing to the imagination. Still as brash today, the Judge ventures out occasionally from his quiet South London hideaway to shock unsuspecting audiences.
Big Six (1972).

JUSTICE, Jimmy
With the help of his backing band – The Excheckers – Justice took his version of the Drifters' hit When My Little Girl Is Smiling to the top ten in 1962. Two more hits followed in the same year but after ten further years of recording without major success he left the music industry. In recent years he has been working as a representitive for a computer company in Surrey.

KAJAGOOGOO

The 1983 single Too Shy proved to be Kajagoogoo's high point before personality differences between spiky haired singer Limahl and songwriter Nick Beggs forced the break up of the band. While the media speculated about the nature of his friendship with Radio One disc jockey Paul Gambaccini, Limahl attempted an unsuccessful solo career – he did manage a No. 4 with the theme song to Never Ending Story.

Nick Beggs still tours playing bass with Gary Numan and until recently was Musical Director to Belinda Carlisle. He had previously worked in the A & R Department at Phonogram records and is now also producing some Japanese acts.

Kajagoogoo

KALLEN, Kitty

How things have changed; Kallen caused a stir in 1955 by appearing at a reception wearing only petticoats. Forty years later hardly an eyebrow is raised at Madonna's choice of attire! The American sweetheart, who is still performing at the age of 71, had been in London promoting her only UK No. 1 when she committed this outrageous act .
Little Things Mean A Lot (1954).

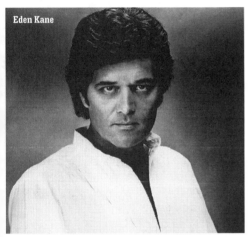

Eden Kane

KANE, Eden

His real name is Richard Sarstedt and he is the brother of Robin and Peter. He reached No. 1 in the summer of 1961 with Well I Ask You and went on to establish a name for himself in Australia, where he became one of the biggest stars on the continent. He blew all his money and in 1970 moved to America hoping to repeat his Australian success and make a name Stateside. He married journalist Charlene Groman, a millionairess, in Los Angeles, where he lives today. Now a resident of California, he spends his time writing songs and occasionally sings in West Coast clubs and lounges. He has also appeared in Star Trek.

KANE GANG

Paul Woods is now working as a sub-editor with the Sunderland Echo. David Brewis and Martin Brammer are still involved in music, writing and performing respectively.
Closest Thing To Heaven (1984).

KATRINA & THE WAVES

300 million people watched this band from Cambridgeshire win the 1997 Eurovision

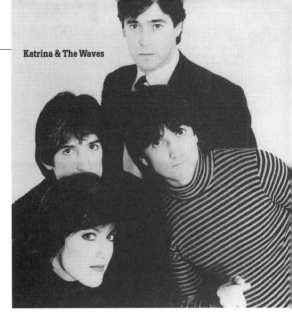

Katrina & The Waves

Song Contest following a twelve year chart absence.
Walking on Sunshine (1985).

KC & The Sunshine Band

The name KC comes courtesy of the surname of the lead singer who is Harry Wayne Casey. In 1981 the group disbanded and KC became a solo artist with Epic Records. After nine years of appearing in the UK charts they finally reached No. 1 with Give It Up in 1983 although Casey had been paralysed in a car crash the year before.
KC's British record label refused to release his hits in America forcing a retirement completely from the music business for a number of years. His father died in 1984 and he started drinking and drug taking resulting in two heart attacks. Now back in full flow, KC and the Sunshine Band can again be seen performing many of their old hits such as Queen of Clubs and Get Down Tonight which was given a new lease of life by being the soundtrack to the Budweiser TV commercials featuring beer guzzling ants!
Give It Up (1983).

KEEGAN, Kevin

Complete with cork-screwed hair Keegan capitalised on his popularity as a footballer to briefly turn pop-star in 1979 and his Head Over Heels In Love reached No 31 thanks to a little help from Smokie. Fortunately his footballing come-backs have been more frequent than his musical ones (he is now involved at Fulham) .

KELLY MARIE

Opportunity Knocks winner at the age of 15 and chart-topper shortly afterwards Kelly Marie settled in north London, marrying in 1984, and going on to have six children which kept her busy during the Eighties. She is now back performing in cabaret and has a single planned for 1997. Her family run a successful dry cleaning business.
Feels Like I'm In Love (1980).

KENNY

The Bump, Fancy Pants and Julie Ann were all top ten hits during 1974 and 1975. Chris Lacklison moved to Cornwall to hire out pleasure boats. Andy Walton ran a studio in South Africa for five years and had his own travel agency before taking a job with LSI Group Leisure (Computers). Chris Redburn now runs Redburn Transfer, one of the UK's largest haulage firms. Yan Style runs his own PA hire firm called Kane Green. Only Richard Driscoll remained with music and experienced further chart success with Cockney Rebel and Classix Nouveaux.

KENNY, Gerard

Received an Ivor Novello award for his composition I Could Be So Good For You, a hit for Dennis Waterman and the theme to ITV series Minder. He also had several solo chart successes himself but never made the top thirty in the UK. Kenny has recently recovered from a serious motor accident to resume live shows which have included providing entertainment on the maiden voyage of the Oriana Liner.

KERSHAW, Nik

A former employee of the Department Of Employment in Ipswich, Kershaw has found himself regular work as a songwriter, singer and producer since the early Eighties. As a spiky haired pop star he managed five top ten's in 1984/5 and has since written hits for numerous artists including Chesney Hawkes' One And Only. Living in a beautiful home in Essex

Nik Kershaw

complete with recording studio, Kershaw is now singer, multi instrumental performer, producer and writer.
I Won't Let The Sun Go Down On Me (1984).

KIDD, Johnny & The Pirates

Johnny Kidd and the Pirate achieved fame in 1961 with the rock n roll classic Shakin' All Over. The Pirates left Kidd to back Tommy Steele's brother before becoming the basis for The Tornadoes and the new Pirates are formed. In 1966 Kidd died in a car crash in Manchester. Guitarist Nick Simper, a member of the new Pirates, survived the crash and eventually became a founder member of Deep Purple. The Pirates carried on performing for a while but split in 1967.

Mick Green worked in Englebert Humperdinck's band before forming Shanghai. As well as re-forming The Pirates in 1976, Green has since played for some of the world biggest artists including Rod Stewart and Paul McCartney.

KING

Paul King (singer) became a VJ on Satellite channel MTV and is now a producer and presenter for music channel VH1. Adrian Lillywhite (drums) remained in the industry as an A & R man. Mick Roberts (keyboards) is now a musical arranger and manages a studio theatre in Coventry.
Love and Pride (1985).

KING, Albert

Inspirational guitarist who was a guiding influence for blues musicians around the world including Eric Clapton and Jimi Hendrix. Died in Memphis aged 69 in 1993.

KING, B B

BB King was already a blues legend when he finally made the British charts with U2 in 1989 with When Love Comes To Town. Now in his late 60s, the big man still manages around 300 concerts a year. He also owns BB King's Blues Club in Memphis.

KING, Ben E

see The DRIFTERS.

King then and Paul King now (below)

KING, Carole

Singer songwriter who in the Sixties formed one of the most successful songwriting partnerships of all time with Jerry Goffen. In the Seventies, boosted by her hugely successful album Tapestry she became a performer of her own song and in the learly Eighties she became one of the first artists to successfully write songs about the environment. In the Nineties King has devoted more time to a career in acting, spending six months starring on Broadway in Blood Brothers in 1994. Royalties continue to flood in from remakes of the Goffen/King classics including Robson and Jerome's version of their Up on the Roof in 1995. *It's Too Late (1971).*

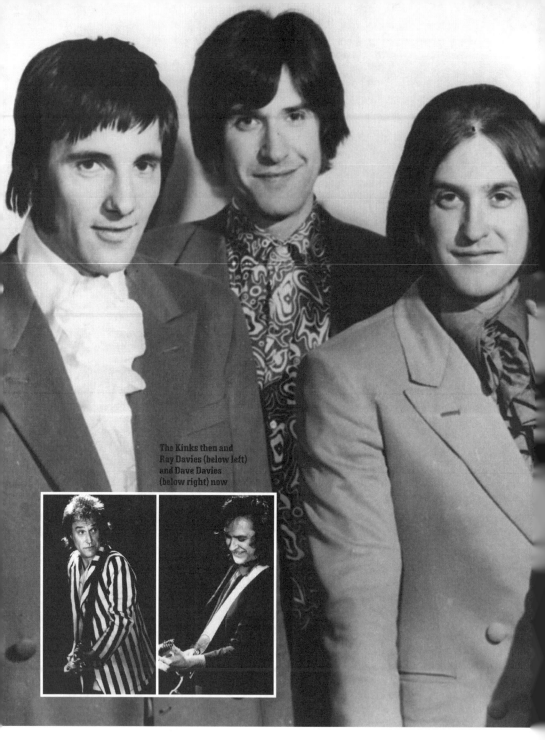

The Kinks then and
Ray Davies (below left)
and Dave Davies
(below right) now

KING CRIMSON

Fronted by Robert Fripp and with Greg Lake
as the original bass guitarist King Crimson
had pedigree and developed a cult following.
In 1984 the band finally split and almost ten
years later in 1983 the group re-formed,
fronted again by Fripp. A new album

released in 1997, was launched at a
gathering in a top London hotel which saw
all the original members in the same room
together for the first time in many years.

Fripp married Toyah Wilcox in 1986 and
John Wetton went on to join supergroups
Asia and UK before touring as a solo artist.

telling anecdotes of his life and times in music. His brother Dave meanwhile released his own book entitled Kink.

Ray toured the USA as a solo performer and even appeared at the 1996 Cambridge Folk Festival. Peter Quaife move to Canada and become an accomplished painter – examples of his work can be seen in an exhibition on the internet.
Lola (1970).

Kathy Kirby

KIRBY, Kathy

One of Britain's best known singers during the early Sixties came second in the Eurovision Song Contest with I Belong. She later gained a reputation for being a prima donna and was eventually made bankrupt owing more than £30,000 to the Inland Revenue. In 1979 she was arrested on a charge of deceiving a London hotel and remanded on bail on the condition that she attended a mental hospital – she was cleared of the charge.

KLF

Former A& R man Bill Drummond and guitarist Jim Cauty decided to give the music business a shake and have become an enigma of the music scene in th eUK. What Time is Love in 1990 became the first hit for

KINKS

The Kinks were fronted by Ray Davies on vocals and brother Dave Davies on guitar. In 1995 Ray Davies' autobiography entitled X-ray is published and later in the same year he had a one-man show called To The Bone on a US tour reading passages from his story and

KLF although they had reached No. 1 two years previously as The Timelords with Doctorin' The Tardis (complete with snippets of Gary Glitter's Rock n Roll Part 2). They have since published a book boasting about how easy it is to have a hit record and were voted top British group at the 1991 BPI awards.

Shortly afterwards they announced rather cryptically that 'Bill Drummond and Jimmy Cauty have now left the music business'. The mystery deepened when they were featured in a 1995 BBC documentary burning a £40,000 painting which they had purchased after it had won the Turner Prize and they also staged the burning of £1 million of their own cash to a huddle of startled journalists.

Bill Drummond is A & R Manager at Warner Brothers and Cauty is now living in Cornwall where he maintains the KLF liking for the unorthodox by using a former army personnel carrier for as his preferred mode of transport.

KNIGHT, Gladys & The Pips

Tamla Motown stalwarts who produced classy soul records for over twenty years. soulsters. Gladys Knight made her acting debut in Pipedream in 1976 and as a solo performer following the band splitting up in 1989 – having just won a Grammy for best R & B performance – she reached the UK top ten with the theme tune from the Bond film Licence To Kill. Original Pip Edward Batten is now wheelchair bound following a stroke in 1995.

Midnight Train To Georgia (1976).

KRAMER, Billy J & The Dakotas

Billy J Krame then (above) and now

Billy J Kramer actually picked the stage name from the Liverpool telephone directory in 1963. In 1966 Kramer left the Dakotas and they finally split in 1968 – Kramer continued his cabaret career as a soloist.

In 1993 Kramer settled in Long Island, New York and is still involved with the Silver Sixties shows. The Dakotas put past differences between them to one side when they played their first gig together for 30 years in April 1997. Kramer reunited with Dakotas including original members Mike Maxfield and Tony Mansfield (Elkie Brooks's brother). Kramer also tours with pick up bands throughout the States. Of the original Dakotas, Ray Jones (bass) became a computer analyst and Robbie McDonald (guitar) took on a pub in Sheffield.

Little Children (1964).

LAINE, Frankie

A Fifties heart-throb who scored his biggest hit with the classic High Noon in 1952. Frankie was still performing live some thirty years later while in his seventies and earning royalties from his record sales which have

Gladys Knight & The Pips

now topped 100 million worldwide. He even managed to appear live only months after a four way heart operation in 1984. Married to film actress Nan Grey, they live in an ocean-front home in San Diego which allows him to indulge in his passion for fishing.

LAKE, Greg
See EMERSON LAKE & PALMER.

LANE, Ronnie
See THE FACES.

Laurel & Hardy

LAUREL and HARDY
The comic duo made about 90 films between 1927-1940. Stan Laurel died in 1965, Oliver Hardy died 1957. Had a belated hit with The Trail Of The Lonesome Pine in 1975.

LAWRENCE, Sophie
Initially left her role as Diane in Eastenders to devote her attentions to a career in pop.

Sophie Lawrence

Despite brief success, she was soon earning £4 per hour as a street canvasser before signing a new deal to return to Albert Square for a considerably higher salary!
Love's Unkind (1991).

Led Zeppelin's Robert Plant

LED ZEPPELIN
Rock giants now part of the digitally re-mastered, re-release original material revival movement. The original line up was Robert Plant (vocals); former Yardbird Jimmy Page (guitar); John Paul Jones (bass); John Bonham (drums).

In 1980 Bonham was found dead in bed at Jimmy Page's house in Windsor, Berkshire having choked in his sleep after a heavy drinking bout. The group then retired for twelve years following Bonham's death. Their mentor Peter Grant, who had also managed The Yardbirds, also then retired from the business and died in 1995 of a heart attack at the age of 60. The three remaining members reunited for Live Aid in 1985, then again in 1988 with Jason Bonham taking his father's place behind the drums. Page and Plant reunited in 1994 and have since taken their unique blend of rock on worldwide tours. Page has a fascination with the occult and in particular the works of Alistair Crowley – he opened a shop selling related items.

Brenda Lee

LEE, Brenda

Five feet tall but packed so much energy Lee was known as Little Miss Dynamite. In 1967 she stopped recording but made a comeback in 1971 with Nobody Wins. She featured on the soundtrack of a 1990 Dick Tracy movie, signed to Warner Brothers in the same year and she has continued to perform throughout the Nineties including a performance at the Elvis Presley birthday banquet at Graceland, Memphis in 1992. Audiences in 52 countries have experienced Little Miss Dynamite in concert and she continues to be a well travelled globe trotter and popular recording artist earning platinum discs even now .She now lives in Nashville with her husband and daughters.
Let's Jump The Broomstick (1961).

LEE, Leapy

Little Arrows was a number 2 for Lee in 1968. However his private life got in the way of mainstream success when he started drinking heavily and mixing with dubios company. He was arrested and jailed following an incident in a Berkshire pub which resulted in the landlord being cut across the wrist. He later moved to Majorca where he took to singing in the local bars and clubs.
Little Arrows (1968).

LEE, Peggy

Singer, lyricist and composer who contributed to jazz, blues, swing, latin and rock music in a long career. Lee had her first million seller in 1948 with Manana, followed by Lover in 1952 and the classic Fever in 1958. She has recorded over 600 songs and 59 albums! She wrote many of the songs for Disney's Lady And The Tramp and played several of the animal characters. She is now in her seventies and confined to a wheelchair following a fall, but is still able to devote considerable energy to worthwhile causes, is still writing songs, books and poems and most remarkably performing live.
Fever (1958).

LEMON PIPERS

Achieved a million seller with Green Tambourine in 1968 but the group split in 1969. Guitarist Bill Bartlett re-emerged many years later in Ram Jam of Black Betty fame.

Lene Lovich

Quirky US vocalist who has worked with Erasure and Belinda Carlisle as well as

At Your Service

Ten with alternative careers

1. Buster Bloodvessell
   Fatty Towers Hotel
2. Fred from Gerry & Pacemakers
   Pacemaker Driving School
3. Chris Farlowe
   Out Of Time Antique shop
4. Rod Argent
   Sheet Music
5. Thump Thompson (Darts)
   Florist
6. Marie Osmond
   Porcelain Dolls
7. Johnny Otis
   Delicatessen
8. Chick Churchill (Ten Years After)
   Art Gallery
9. Bill Wyman
   Sticky Fingers Restaurant
10. Bertie Higgins
    Rum Runners Bar

Jerry Lee Lewis then (main pic)
and with Dennis Quaid (above)

recording as a solo artist over the late-Seventies early-Eighties. Lovich is mainly into non-musical projects these days and was reported to be writing a vampire/western novel and a collection of short stories. *Lucky Number (1979).*

LENNON, John
See The BEATLES.

LEWIE, Jona
See TERRY DACTYL & THE DINOSAURS.

LEWIS, Jerry Lee
One of the most colourful rock n roll careers which since the Fifties has encapsulated drugs, booze and marriage to a thirteen year old – as well as some of the best live performances of his time. Tragedy also touched his backing band when one member died prematurely in a car crash and another died in a drowning accident. Despite his chequered personal life in 1986 he was given the honour of being the first artist to be inducted into Rock n Roll Hall of Fame. In the

1989 film of his life, inevitably entitled Great Balls Of Fire, Dennis Quaid played the starring role. In 1993 his autobiography Killer was published and 1997 saw him on his 40th anniversary world tour.
Great Balls Of Fire (1957).

John Leyton

LEYTON, John

A former rep actor whose appearance in TV's Harper's West One – singing Johnny Remember Me resulted in the station's phones being jammed by teenage girls wanting to find out about their new star – 18,000 of them supposedly joined his fan club!

After subsequent singles failed to make the same impact he returned full time to acting and appeared in films including the Great Escape and Von Ryan's Express. Since 1992 he has worked in the catering industry running a restaurant in London's Portobello Road (Market Bar on Portobello Road) and previously ran the Meridiana before selling for redevelopment. In 1994 he once again took to the live stage, joining a Fifties revival tour (Solid Gold Rock N Roll) and has appeared regularly ever since.
Johnny Remember Me (1961).

LIEUTENANT PIGEON

The group was called Stavely Makepeace but chose Lieutenant Pigeon for their 1972 novelty hit Mouldy Old Dough. They released ten more singles before splitting in 1988 and re-forming briefly in 1992. Steve Johnson now has own home recording studio and runs a company called Mediatrax.

Hilda, Steve's mum, whose front room was used for the recording of Mouldy Old Dough and made famous in the video, has now moved out and enjoys the quieter life associated with 82 year olds.

Drummer Nigel Fletcher had a passion for trains and became a signalman but now earns his living doing research (including information for a train buff documentary Video On Steam.
Mouldy Old Dough (1972).

LIGHT OF THE WORLD

Eighties band who in their prime were described as "the epitome of British funky soul sound". They disbanded after a number of hit albums to form groups such as

Lindisfarne

David Grant
of Linx now

Incognito (Always There – No. 6 in 1991) and Beggar & Co before reforming in 1996 to tour the clubs.

LIMAHL
See KAJAGOOGOO.

LINDISFARNE
Ray Jackson, Simon Crowe, Rod Clements and Ray Laidlaw comprised the original members. Jackson left to work in PR; Simon Crowe left to run a brewery in Canada; Laidlaw is now band manager as well as drummer. Despite the death of principal songwriter Alan Hull, the group's electric/acoustic style continues to attract large audiences whenever the current line up appear. Old top ten hits such as Lady Elanor and Fog On The Tyne rekindle memories of the classic Lindisfarne years. Hull had also established himself as a solo artist and had just completed the vocal tracks on a new album when he suffered a fatal heart attack at the age of 50 on 17th November 1995.
Lady Eleanor (1972).

LINX
Singer David Grant went solo and hit the charts himself and in duets with Jaki Graham. In 1988 made a documentary about children in poverty. He

is currently involved in gospel singing, acting and is still touring.

LIQUID GOLD
Last seen on Top Of The Pops with mad drummer Wole Rothe dressed in a caveman's outfit. Both he and the group's guitarist Syd Twynham now form part of Les Gray's revival of Seventies throwbacks Mud.
Dance Yourself Dizzy (1980).

LITTLE EVA
One time baby sitter for Carole King. It is now thirty five years since The Loco-motion first hit the dance floors and twenty five years since its last re-appearance in the charts. However, it still has the same motivating impact when spun by modern day disc jockeys. Eva still performs the occasional live performance having spent a time out of the industry including a spell working as a waitress.
Loco-motion (1962).

LITTLE RICHARD
Recorded half a dozen classics and etched his name in music history before his beliefs encouraged him to leave the music business to study religion at Oakland Adventist College. A Seventh Day Adventist, he later went by the name of The Georgia Peach working for a number of years as a minister.
Long Tall Sally (1957).

Little Richard

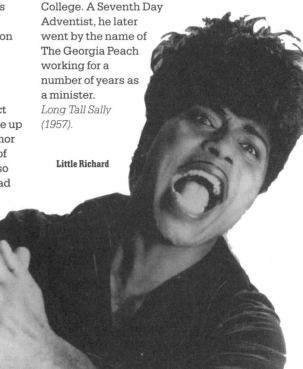

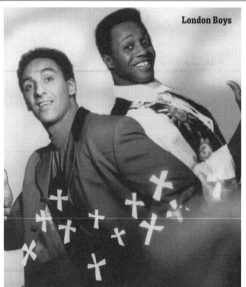

London Boys

LOBO

Roland Kent Lavoire named the band after his dog.He carved out an enormously successful career writing radio and television jingles and recording demo-tapes in his home studio. He later produced Spiders & Snakes for Jim Stafford and is now signed to a Japanese based record label and has been touring Asia.
Me And You And A Dog Named Boo (1971).

LONDON BOYS

Pop duo Eden Ephraim and Dennis Fuller died in a car crash in the Alps on January 21st 1996. They had continued to be successful in Europe but not made any British impact since London Nights made No.2 in 1989.

LOPEZ, Trini

Known for his Sixties hit If I had a Hammer he was also in the film The Dirty Dozen. He was charged with beating his former girlfriend Rose Mihata but was only convicted of one minor charge because Lopez did not have a prior criminal record.

LOUDERMILK, John D

Only UK chart placing was in 1962 with The Language Of Love but has a sound pedigree as a songwriter– penning songs like Tobacco Road and Indian Reservation. He lives in Nashville and has an unusual hobby – he is a devoted hurricane chaser and travels up and down when notified of a predicted storm!

LOVE AFFAIR

Big with the mods, Love Affair scored five consecutive top twenty singles fronted by Steve Ellis. He later had spells with Ellis and Widowmaker (which also featured former members of Mott The Hoople, Hawkwind and Lindisfarne). After recovering from a serious accident he continued to write songs and in 1992 was persuaded to form Steve Ellis' Love Affair due to the constant airplay of their biggest hit Everlasting Love (No. 1 in 1968). This caused a legal rumpus as former band member Martin Lyon had created and managed a new Love Affair. Both parties have now agreed that there is room for two versions of the band to co-exsist despite the confusion.

LOVIN' SPOONFUL

Formed by half of the Mamas and Papas. Yanovsky had problems with drugs and tried a solo career. John Sebastian moved to Los Angeles and appeared at Woodstock, playing acoustic guitar amid the notorious downpour. He penned a No. 1 hit in 1976 with Welcome Back, the theme to John Travolta's American TV series, became television presenter, wrote a children's book and wrote the music for the Care Bears cartoon.

Lulu

LULU

Marie McDonald McLaughlin Lawrie was fifteen years old and still at school when she had a hit with Shout. Her marriage to Bee Gee Maurice Gibb lasted six years before ending in divorce in 1975. In 1980 she starred in the international TV series Let's Rock and in various TV shows on both sides of the Atlantic. More recently she has appeared with teen sensations Take That. Now remarried, she lived with her hairdresser husband John Frieda and son Jordan, in London.

LYMON, Frankie & Teenagers

In 1956 Why do Fools Fall in Love? became a No. 1 in England and Frankie Lymon became a teenage heart-throb. The following year he broke away from the Teenagers although they carried on in their own right. In 1960 he entered a drug rehabilitation programme but in 1964 he was arrested and found guilty of narcotics offences. In 1968 Lymon's body was discovered in his grandmother's New York house where he grew up prompting newspaper headlines of "Star at 13 but dead at the age of 25". Two original members of the Teenagers are now also dead: Joe Negroni died in 1978 from a cerebral haemorrhage; Sherman Garnes died in prison in 1977. In 1992 a court ruled that the remaining two members, Herman Santiago and Jimmy Merchant (Merchant was employed as a taxi driver at the time) were entitled to back-dated royalties for Why do Fools Fall in Love? along with Frank Lymon's widow – estimated at $4 million over 38 years.

LYNCH, Kenny

After a tring of sixties hits this close buddy of Jimmy Tarbuck with whom he can now often be found either in cabaret or appearing on the local golf course. Co-wrote the Small Faces No. 1, Sha La La Lee.

LYNRYD SKYNYRD

Ronnie Van Zant who had a reputation for bar-room brawls and Steve Gaines, one of the band's guitarists, died in 1977 when the plane that they were travelling in crashed into a swamp in Gilsberg, Massachusetts. The remainder of the band were all seriously injured but eventually recovered to go on to form a new career with the Russington Collins Band. In 1986 Allen Collins, the group's guitarist, is paralysed when his car runs off the road. Later in the same year Lynryd Skynyrd were persuaded to re-form but in 1990 Collins died in Jacksonville Memorial Medical Centre having been in hospital since 1989.

In 1992 Artimus Pyle was arrested at his Jacksonville beach home on the charge of sexually assaulting a fyoung girl and is held without bail. The following year he was sentenced to eight years probation for molesting two sisters after pleading guilty to attempted battery and lewd and lascivious assault.

In the same year the Ronnie Van Zant Memorial Park opens in Clay County, Florida (the are he grew up in) as a recreation area for children. Ricky Medlocke has now rejoined the new version of the band with Johnny Van Zant on vocals following the split of Blackfoot. *Free Bird (1976).*

McCARTNEY, Paul
See The BEATLES.

McCOYS, The
Their 1965 single Hang On Sloopy was a million-selling single all over the world. They later became the backing group for the albino rock n roller Johnny Winter. Rick Zehringer (guitar) changed his stage name to Derringer in 1970 and went on to have a hit with the Edgar Winter Band with the instrumental Frankenstein as well as being a successful solo artist in his own right. Steely Dans' song Rikki Don't Lose That Number is about Derringer. He is now a popular session musician and producer.

McCOY, Van
World-wide success as a performing artist in 1975 with the million-selling American chart-topping disco single The Hustle. Van McCoy was well established and respected in music circles as a record-producer and songwriter with his companies Van McCoy Productions and Vanda Records, in 1967. By the early Seventies he was producing and arranging

for The Stylistics. He died, tragically, at the height of his personal recording success.

McFADDEN & WHITEHEAD
Gene McFadden and John Whitehead wrote and performed Ain't No Stoppin Us Now (No. 5 in May 1979) which sold over eight million copies and was nominated for a grammy award. The duo are still performing together in their native America.

McLEAN, Don
American folk singer whi is besy known for American Pie and Vincent. He is now living in Maine with his wife and two children, working on his autobiography and recording for Cerb Records.
Vincent (1972).

Suggs now (above) and the whole of Madness (below)

McGUINNESS FLINT
See MANFRED MANN.

McGUIRE, Barry
AT the height of America's VietNam protest era McGuire sneaked to No. 1 with his controversial anti-war protest song Eve Of Destruction. Achieving only moderate success thereafter, he became a Christian evangelist and has devoted his life to his religious beliefs and recorded only gospel albums ever since.

McKENZIE, Scott
The era of flower power is synonymous with McKenzie's San Francisco (Be Sure To Wear Some Flowers In Your Hair. The American singer faded away with the hippy era and dropped out to live in the desert and went around barefoot talking to cactus plants. He then lived in Virginia Beach for over 10 years (which he claims is inhabited by psychics and weirdos!). Not seen for many years on the music scene he unexpectedly emerged as a 'papa' in a new version of The Mamas and The Papas.

McLACHLAN, Craig
Former Neighbours actor who moved to Britain in 1990 and reached No. 2 in the charts with Mona. He maintained a high profile with his acting, starring in BBCTV's Bugs, and he also took a turn playing Danny in the stage version of Grease from which he managed two further chart hits with his co-star Debbie Gibson.

MADNESS
This group of musical funsters ruled the charts in the early Eighties. In 1986 the group officially split and the former members headed off in various directions.

Mark Bedford (bass player) completed a Printers and Designers Course at college and works in graphic design as well as working on film scores.

Mike Barson went into semi-retirement in Amsterdam but is now writing again with Suggs. Woody Woodgate (drums) continues to collaborate with the Voice Of The Beehive and has his own band called FAT – an acronym for 'fuck all that'!

Carl Smyth (Chas Smash) became A & R manager at Go! Discs and has his own

Honoured
Ten who have had official recognition

1 Sir Bob Geldof
2 Sir Cliff Richard
3 Lord David Dundas
4 Sir Paul McCartney
5 Rest of the Beatles – MBE
6 The Goodies – all OBE
7 The Goons, Sir Harry Seycombe, Spike Milligan OBE
8 Kenny Lynch OBE
9 Honourable Sue Nicholls
10 Screaming Lord Sutch

company called Quite Man Management based in north London. Sax player Kix has a band called Crunch with Crissy Boy (guitar).

Suggs (lead singer) became a regular comedy host at The Mean Fiddler club in north London before managing The Farm. In 1995 he signed to East-West Records as a solo artist in 1996 hit No. 4 in the UK chart with a revival of Paul Simon's Cecilia. Suggs is now signed to Warner Brothers and presents for Channel 5 TV.
House Of Fun (1982).

MAISONETTES, The
See CITY BOY.

MAMAS & THE PAPAS
Fronted by Mama Cass they had hit singles with California Dreaming and Monday, Monday, in the mid-Sixties. Band member John Phillips penned San Francisco (Be Sure To Wear Some Flowers in your Hair) for Scott McKenzie. The band dissolved in 1968 and re-formed for one concert in 1971.

John Phillips based himself at his Malibu home and in 1981 was jailed for five years for drugs offences, later commuted to community service. He underwent a liver transplant in 1995 after a life of drug abuse. His daughter Chynna entered the music business and succeeded with Wilson Phillips (Hold On, No. 6 in 1990).

Mama Cass turned to cabaret and then back to acting. She was found dead at Harry Nillson's London flat on July 29, 1974, just after completing a successful season at the London Palladium. She was 32 and had suffered from a heart attack.

Michelle Phillips appeared in Ken Russell's Valentino and was romantically linked with Easy Rider star Dennis Hopper after her divorce from Phillips – she later spent three years with Warren Beatty. She also re-released her own California Dreaming and prevented a film being made about the life and times of the band.

Doherty went solo but failed to recapture his early success and drifted into obscurity.

A new version of the band is gigging with former Spanky & Our Gang lead singer Elaine McFarlane

California Dreaming (1966).

MANFRED MANN

Manfred Mann, Paul Jones, Mike Hugg, Tom McGuinness and singer Mike D'Abo had a succession of hits in the mid Sixties. They disbanded in 196 and two years later Mann formed Manfred Mann's Earthband who went on to enjoy hits with Joy Bringer and Blinded By The Light.

Mike Vickers left the group to branch out on a solo career during which he penned many film and TV show soundtracks. He was replaced by Jack Bruce (see Cream) who played bass while Tom McGuinness switched to guitar. Bruce stayed with Manfred Mann for only six months.

Guitarist Tom McGuinness formed his own group, teaming up with former John Mayall's Blues-breaker Hughie Flint to front McGuinness Flint. McGuinness and Flint came back into the commercial limelight as part of the successful group The Blues Band with singer Paul Jones who earlier had a successful solo career with I've Been A Bad, Bad, Boy (1967) and his debut hit High Time in 1966.

He returned to stage work appearing in Cats and later in television shows. He also presents a blus show on BBC Radio 2.

D'Arbo of Manfred now

Benny Gallagher and Graham Lyle had two British hit singles – When I'm Dead and Gone and Malt And Barley Blues.

Jones, D'Abo, Mike Hugg, Tom McGuinness, Mike Vickers plus Benny Gallagher and Rob Townshend were touring as the Manfreds in 1997 and a new album is planned.

Pretty Flamingo (1966).

MANHATTANS

American vocal group named after a cocktail (not after the area of New York). The band was formed while the members were serving with the United States Air Force based in Germany. They still perform today although original singer George 'Smitty' Smith died in 1970 from spinal meningitis.

Kiss And Say Goodbye (1976).

Bob Marley

MARLEY, Bob & The Wailers

Still regarded as the ultimate reggae artist and revered in God-like fashion in his native Jamaica. Marley died in 1981 from lung cancer and a brain tumour at the age of 36 at the Cedars Olive Hospital. In 1987 Carlton Barrett, the band's drummer, was shot dead outside his home in Kingston, Jamaica and later in the same year Peter Tosh, singer and guitarist, was also murdered, but by burglars, at his Jamaican home. Marley has a statue erected in his honour in his home

village and there is a museum dedicated to his memory in Kingston.
No Woman, No Cry (1975).

Marmalade's Secrets Club

MARMALADE

Ob-La-Di Ob-La-Da stayed at No. 1 for twenty weeks during 1968-69.

Junior Campbell left in 1971, had a solo hit with Hallelujah Freedom and wrote theme tunes for many television programmes including Thomas The Tank Engine and Tugs.

In 1975 Dean Ford left the group and emigrated to America to drive luxury taxis. He was joined in the States by Patrick Fairley who went into publishing before opening his own watering hole called The Scotland Yard.

Graham Knight (bass guitarist) and Alan Whitehead (drummer) resurrected the name Marmalade in 1976 and had a top ten hit the following year with Falling Apart at the Seams. The current line up still includes Knight.

Alan Whitehead now owns Secrets, a club in Hammersmith which gained national publicity when neighbour BBC broadcaster John Humphreys complained about the entertainment being provided – lap dancing. Sandy Newman fronts the current Marmalade who have proved to be one of the most popular re-vitalised Sixties bands on the circuit.

MARTELL, Lena

Popular cabaret singer who hit the top spot in 1979 with One Day At A Time. Martell retired completely from music in the late Eighties.

MARTHA & The Muffins

Returned to Canada and shortened the name to M & M. The group consisted of two Marthas; Martha Ladly took a degree in Fine Art before taking control of Real World Records' design department; Martha Johnson writes film scores and TV themes while her husband (the band's guitarist) works in garden design.
Echo Beach (1980).

MARTHA (REEVES) & The Vandellas

American all girl group whose first entered the UK charts in 1964 with Dancing In The Street (covered by David Bowie and Mick Jagger 21 years later). However, it was when the song was re-issued in 1969 that they finally made the top ten. Martha Reeves split from the Vandellas following a bitter legal battle in 1971 to start a solo career. Annette Sterman went on to work in a hospital and Rosalind Ashford for a telephone company, although they occasionally came out of their semi-retirement to perform with Reeves. Sandra Tilley, the other Vandella, died in 1982 having already retired from the music business.

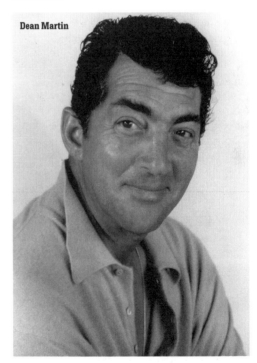

Dean Martin

MARTIN, Dean

Former prize fighter who liked a drop of the hard stuff, Martin succeeded as a romantic singer, actor and comedy side-kick to Jerry Lewis. He achieved eleven top ten hits in

England in the Fifties and Sixties, notably Memories Are Made Of This and Gentle On My Mind. He died on Christmas Day 1995 at Beverly Hills, California.

MARTINDALE, Wink

Jackson based disc jockey Martindale charted on five separate occasions between 1959 and 1973, remarkably all with the same song – Deck of Cards. Has now devoted his energy to acting, no doubt while waiting for the next re-release, and is a game show host on American TV.

MARTINO, Al

Best known for his massive hit Spanish Eyes Al Martino also scored a No. 1 with his first ever release Here in My Heart in 1952. In 1971 he appeared as Johnny Fontaine in the film The Godfather, a rather ironic twist of fate as it is claimed that earlier in his career Martino fell foul of the Mafia and had to flee to England. Periods of despair led to drug and drink addiction and in 1979 he was convicted of shoplifting. Happily, this has not dampened his popularity and he is now back in America living in some splendour in Beverly Hills.

MARVELETTES, The

Please Mr Postman provided Tamla Motown with their first No. 1 and was the label's second only million seller! It was not until the Carpenters released their version of the song that it became known in Britain. By the end of

Al Martino

the Sixties the Marvalettes had effectively finished; Georgeanna Tillman was forced to retire through ill-health; Juanita Cowart and Gladys Horton also left. A version of the band has continued to perform as an R & B outfit.

MARVIN, Hank

See THE SHADOWS.

MASON, Barry

The songwriter who wrote Delilah, Love Grows and many more hits. He now lives in north London where he is working on a new musical and still occasionally appears live.

Graham Fenton of Matchbox

MATCHBOX

Found a niche in the market with their rockabilly style in the early Eighties when the public tired of punk music. Fifteen years on the original five members of the band have reunited, prompted by the response to a on-off gig in London. Lead singer Graham Fenton recently toured with 1957/8 line up of Gene Vincent's band and had continued as a solo artist while his colleagues had taken up alternative employment. Gordon still works as a technician on the Buddy stage show.
When You Ask About Love (1980).

MATTHEWS' SOUTHERN COMFORT

Iain Matthews was formerly with Fairport Convention. He worked in A & R at Island Records before moving to California. He has now resumed writing, after being advised to do so by Robert Plant, and sung on Nancy Griffiths recent albums.
Woodstock (1970).

M

MATHIS, Johnny

Celebrated forty years as a recording artist in 1996. He tours nationally and internationally and has appeared at US Presidential state dinners and Royal Command Performances. He still records an album a year. He is a keen golfer who can boast a single figure handicap and the feat of a hole-in-one on four occasions.

When A Child Is Born (1976).

MAUGHAN, Susan

Wanted to be Bobby's Girl in 1960 and nearly forty years later she is still touring and appearing in pantomime.

MAY, Brian

See QUEEN.

MAYFIELD, Curtis

Mayfield left Sixties American soul band The Impressions in 1971 and almost immediately scored a UK hit with Move On Up (it was not until four years later that his former colleagues charted with First Impressions). In 1983 they again joined forces for a successful 25th anniversary tour and three of the original members still perform together in cabaret. Mayfield has recovered from almost total paralysis (following an on-stage accident in 1990) to record New World Order in 1997.

MEDICINE HEAD

John Fiddler and Peter Hope-Evans reached No. 3 in 1973 with One And One Is One. In 1976 Fiddler joined the British Lions with surviving members of Mott (previously Mott The Hoople) following the break up of both groups. Fiddler linked up again in the mid-Eighties with Yardbirds survivors to form Box Of Frogs and was later part of a new version of the Yardbirds. He continues with his solo career and sang with Joe Cocker in the early Nineties. Peter Hope-Evans worked on Pete Townshend's White City soundtrack in 1985.

One And One Is One (1973).

MELANIE

Melanie Safka emerged from the Woodstock festival as Melanie, the star. She is now living in Clearwater, Florida where she has formed her own Neighbourhood record label. In 1980 she joined the Woodstock 20th anniversary reunion tour and is still performing but these days more for charity and in cabaret.

Brand New Key (1972).

MELVIN, Harold, & The Bluenotes

Harold Melvin started singing on Philadelphia street corners years ago and the group became a stalwart of the Philly Sound. Although they have undergone many personnel changes, the group continued to perform until Harold Melvin died from a heart attack on 24th March 1997 at the age of 57.

If You Don't Know Me By Now (1973).

Harold Melvin & The Bluenotes

MEN AT WORK

In 1983 Aussie anthem Down Under was a UK No. 1 after striking a chord in Australia. Two years later the group disbanded. In 1996 Colin Hay, the lead singer, set up an Australian record label called Lazy Eye. He spends half his time in Oz and the remainder in a Californian town called Topanga which provided the title to the first of his five subsequent solo albums. He has now also embarked on an acting career.

MERCURY, Freddie

See QUEEN.

MERSEYBEATS

They disbanded in 1966, with only Crane and Kinsley staying on from the original group.

Marseybeats

Middle of the Road then (above) and now

The two of them resurfaced shortly afterwards as The Merseys and had a hit with Sorrow in 1966. Crane re-formed The Merseybeats as Tony Crane And The Merseybeats while Kinsley created Liverpool Express and charted with You are my Love, Hold Tight and Dreamin in the mid Seventies. Now known as LEX, they continue to tour Britain and Europe.

However, the Merseybeats are still going strong under the joint guidance of Crane and Kinsley, regularly appearing in cabaret as well as touring Europe – in 1993 they celebrated their 30th anniversary. For the past two years they have been voted best live group by readers of The Beat Goes On with Crane being voted best vocalist.

The original guitarist Aaron Williams runs his own engineering business (Tony Crane married his sister Carol).
I Think Of You (1964).

MIDDLE OF THE ROAD

Hot Pants helped male temperatures soar during the summer of 1971 while Middle Of The Road topped the pop charts with Chirpy Chirpy Cheep Cheep. Fronted by Sally Carr they enjoyed immense popularity earning thirty-two gold discs for Cheep Cheep and their follow up single Tweedle Dee Tweedle Dum. Having been off the scene for fifteen

years, they re-emerged in 1991 and have been touring regularly around Europe ever since. Today, under the banner of Sally Carr's Middle Of The Road, Sally sings with original drummer Ken Andrew and original guitarist Neil Henderson.

MILES, John

Guitarist who recorded two smashes in the mid Seventies with Music and High Fly is now a member of Tina Turner's backing band

MILLER, Roger

After several big British hits in the Sixties, most notably Little Green Apples and England Swings, Miller opened an hotel in Nashville named after his 1965 No. 1 King Of The Road. He wrote the score for the Broadway version of Mark Twain's Huckleberry Finn and won an award for Best Musical. He continued thereafter to be successful as a country singer. He died of cancer in 1992 in Century City Hospital, Los Angeles.
King of the Road (1965).

MILLIE

Millie was just sixteen years old when My

Boy Lollipop almost topped the charts in 1964. She then disappeared from the pop scene almost as quickly as she had arrived. She now claims that 'I haven't needed to work since then', although she did appear nude in a mens magazine before devoting her life to 'the service of Christ, speaking His word, and spreading His gospel'.

MILLI VANILLI

Created by Boney M mentor Frank Farian, Milli Vanilli were massively successful until it was revealed that the two supposed members – Rob Pilatus and Fabrice Morvan – did not sing on their hits.

MINDBENDERS

See WAYNE FONATANA AND THE MINDBENDERS.

MINOGUE Kylie

Another of the Australian soap Neighbours participants who turned pop star but with more success than the others (perhaps Jason Donovan apart) put together. The late Eighties were the golden years in terms of chart success for teen idol Kylie who has since matured as a classy singer.

I Should Be So Lucky (1988).

MIRACLES

See SMOKEY ROBINSON.

MITCHELL, Guy

1997 marked two landmarks for Guy Mitchell; he celebrated both his 70th birthday and fifty years as a successful recording artist. His 1956 disc of Singing The Blues is Columbia Records' biggest selling single release ever with world-wide sales in excess of 10 million. Out of over 30 hits, six earned Gold Discs for sales over 1 million copies and five were British

Guy Mitchell

number ones. One of the few artists who can boast success over five decades, he even now has the support of an active appreciation society'. However, Guy has had more than his share of personal problems; two divorces, illness and injuries all took their toll and by the mid Seventies he went into semi-retirement to concentrate on ranching although he does venture out for the occasional live appearance.

MITCHELL, Joni

Canadian folk singer whose commercial heyday came and went with the love and peace hippy era. Now lives in middle America where she devotes most of her time to painting and the occasional tour and infrequent new record.

Big Yellow Taxi (1970).

MODERN ROMANCE

Part of the New Romantics fad of the early Eighties. Geoff Deanne (singer) left in 1982, when he wrote Divine's hit You Think You're A Man. He is now a comedy writer for TV. David Jaymes went into band management and his brother Robbie went into advertising. John Du Prez writes film scores which have included the three Teenage Mutant Hero Turtle films. He also co-wrote the theme to popular TV comedy series One Foot In the Grave with Eric Idle. The remaining member Andy Kynacou can now be found playing his drums at Greek weddings.

MOJOS

Having secured a recording deal with Decca by winning a talent show, The Mojos broke into the top ten with Everything's Alright in 1964. Later releases never matched their early success and the band eventually split in 1966. Singer Stu James pursued a career in music publishing while later members Aynsley Dunbar and Lewis Collins achieved even greater notoriety. Dunbar has since beat his drums for a host of stars and Collins made his name as an actor through the character Bodie in the TV series The Professionals.

Kylie Minogue

MONKEES

A somewhat artificially created band formed specifically to star in the television series of the same name; this didn't prevent them selling over 3 million copies of their debut album. The happy-go-lucky public image disguised much dissatisfaction behind the scenes which resulted in Peter Tork's departure in 1968 which cost him a reputed $160,000 to be released from his contract. The other three wanted to follow suit but were put off by the cost, although they did finally disband in 1970. In 1971 Tork spent four months in prison for possession of marijuana; he later became a teacher and then a waiter.

Mike Nesmith earned a solo contract and went on to form the Pacific Arts Corporation, releasing records and books. In 1979 Mike Nesmith's mother earned herself a staggering $47million from the sale of her patent for a liquid paper (similar to Tippex), but died the following year leaving the entire fortune to her son.

Davy Jones concentrated on acting (having once appeared in Coronation Street as Ena Sharples' grandson) and indulged in his passion for horses; he managed to combine both in the BBC TV series Trainer. In 1995 he finally won his first big race at Lingfield riding his horse Big Race.

Micky Dolenz became a showbiz director responsible for the stage show Bugsy Malone and the television programme Metal Mickey being amongst his successes. He also had a book published in 1983 entitled I'm a Believer: My Life of Monkees' Music and Madness. Dolenz has since taken up painting and has had his first solo art show in Philadelphia.

A UK tour in 1997 re-united all four members but was not the success that was hoped for.

THE MONKS

See THE STRAWBS.

MONRO, Matt

A stable mate of the Beatles at Parlophone Records in the Sixties, although at the other end of the chart spectrum. He enjoyed a succession of hits but is most readily remembered for his recording of the title tune to the film Born Free, which only charted when successfully copied by Vic Reeves in 1991. Monro died from cancer in 1985.

Bankrupt!

Ten who have experienced bankruptcy

1. Gary Glitter
2. Desmond Dekker
3. Vanilla Ice
4. MC Hammer
5. Kevin Rowland
6. Marvin Gaye
7. Andy Gibb
8. Isaac Hayes
9. P.J. Proby
10. Sly Stone

MONTEZ, Chris

His international hit song Let's Dance still provides a living for Sixties star Montez. The audiences at the cabaret clubs where he has been performing for many years may well remember dancing to its first release in 1962 and still jump to their feet today, although their hips swivel a little slower these days. *Let's Dance (1962).*

MOODY BLUES

Originally formed in 1964 by members of several Birmingham based R & B bands, The Moody Blues instantly scored a No. 1 single with Go Now, but it was their change of musical style to blend rock with classical music that established them as a a world wide force. Justin Heyward, John Lodge, Ray Thomas and Graham Edge have now been together since 1978 when the band re-formed after a four year split.

Of the other original membership, Denny Laine went on to form a major part in Paul McCartney's Wings. Clint Warwick (bass) left in 1965 and has kept out of the music business ever since. Mike Pinder who left in 1978 worked as a consultant for Atari Computers before re-emerging in the early Nineties with two albums and is currently working on the third in a trilogy of children's records called An Earth With One Spirit.

Former Yes keyboard player Patrick Moraz, who briefly joined in 1991 but tried to sue the group for half a million dollars for alleged breach of contract when they decided not to keep him on, is now a solo artist and film composer. *Nights In White Satin (1972).*

MOORE, Gary
See THIN LIZZY.

MOTORS, The
Nick Garvey who had also been a member of Ducks Deluxe went into A& R with Polydor, but is now a house husband tinkering with occasional new songs at home. Guitarist Bram Tchaikovsky was last seen working in a pub. Ricky Slaughter (drums) had his house burned down in the Brixton riots then ctook a degree in jazz and pop composition.
Airport (1978).

MOTT THE HOOPLE
Fronted by Ian Hunter and Mick Ralphs (guitarist) who left to join Bad Company when Hunter took control of band. When the band parted in 1974 Hunter and Mick Ronson joined forces for a while before pursuing solo careers. Ian Hunter produced Generation X and in 1977 wrote the modern pop classic Reflections Of A Rock n Roll Star which has now been re-published by Independent Music Press after 15 years out of print. Hunter recorded ten solo albums and moved to New York in 1990; he now lives in Connecticut. His son Jess acted in the film Sleepers with Robert DeNiro. Hunter released a new album and single on Citadel in 1997.

Mick Ronson died in 1993 of liver cancer in London. Morgan Fisher Watts and Griffin stayed through the Mott days but split in the late-Seventies. Griffin became a Radio 1 producer of sessions by new band then played keyboards on Queen's 1982 tour before travelling extensively and settling in Japan where he built the Handmade Studio and had his own Abstract Photographic Exhibition. He has since performed with numerous Japanese artists both live and on record and TV commercials and composed the music for the Fourth International Whale and Dolphin conference in Tokyo. He had a book published in 1995 – the Far East Tour Diary – and in 1996 released a Mott Tribute album featuring some of Japan's biggest bands. Ariel Bender, who briefly replaced Mick Ralphs, has recently released a new solo album under his real name – Luther Grosvenor – after being out of music for fifteen years during which time he worked in an electrical shop, in removals and for a decorating firm that he still runs.

MOUSKOUURI Nana
Female vocalist from Greece who later became Culture Minister for the Greek government and campaigned for England to return the Elgin Marbles.
Only Love (1986).

MOVE
Carl Wayne, Roy Wood, Chris 'Ace' Kefford, Trevor Burton and Bev Bevan made up the Move. Their Flowers in the Rain was the first record to be played on BBC Radio One.

Carl Wayne (who is married to Crossroads' Miss Diane, Susan Hanson) attempted a solo singing career in 1970 and also starred in his own television series Anglia TV. He spent six years as the narrator in Blood Brothers and won a Gold disc for his contribution to the Andrew Lloyd Webber Collection album.

Wayne was replaced by Jeff Lynne but just a few months later, The Electric Light Orchestra was formed – Lynne and Bev Bevan remained with ELO and drummer Bevan formed ELO Part II.

Roy Wood created Wizzard and hit the charts with seven massive singles between December 1972 and December 1974 which included British chart-toppers See My Baby Jive and Angel Fingers' During Wizzard's short-lived success, Roy Wood also established his own solo recording career with such hits as Dear Elaine, Forever and Oh What a Shame. The group split in 1975. Roy Wood now works with the Roy Wood Big Band comprising eleven members.

Rick Price quit to take over as personal assistant-cum-road manager to the British

Mott The Hoople

(From left) Mungo Jerry's Colin Earl, Paul King and Ray Dorset

singing duo Peters and Lee. He works also as personal assistant to British comedian, Jim Davidson. Ace Kefford re-emerged at Cropredy festival 1997 after many troubled years in retirement from the music business.

Jeff Lynne has been in dispute with record company Warner Brotherswhich held up a solo album and the third Willburys album. He has also worked as producer for Tom Jones, Hank Marvin and the Beatles.

Trevor Burton in still active on the Brum music scene with his own band.
Blackberry Way (1968).

Mud

MUD

Formed in Mitcham in 1966 and had the country dancing with Tiger Feet in the early Seventies as a light rock n roll alternative to the prevailing glam rock scene. In 1977 the group split with lead singer Les Gray having a minor hit as a solo artist. Ex-drummer Dave Mount, who at one time was tipped for acting

stardom, hit harder times, went bankrupt and now lives in Croydon. He has worked selling kitchens and more recently as an insurance salesman.

Gray is still on the scene fronting Les Gray's Mud. Ray Stiles is now bass guitarist with the Hollies and Rob Davis has become a successful producer.
Lonely This Christmas (1974).

MUNGO JERRY

In The Summertime sold an astonishing 23 million copies and topped the charts across Europe. The band was almost called D'Jurann D'Jurann – the other favoured choice when guitarist Paul King suggested names for the band.

When the group disbanded Ray Dorset, the singer with the mass of curly hair and extraordinary sideboards, continued in the form of Mungo. Now over 25 years later and the father of five children, he still manages to find time to perform and has continued to tour both in the UK and in Europe keeping the name of Mungo Jerry very much alive. He wrote Feels Like I'm In Love for Elvis Presley shortly before the King died. Dorset has written TV song's for Paul Daniels' Wizbit and the theme to the TV show Prospects. He now lives in Bournemouth where he at one time had five cars including an Aston Martin and a Bentley.

Keyboards player Colin Earl is now a classic car doctor living in Weybridge, Surrey and he restores old cars as well as indulging in his passion for Ferraris.

Paul King is taking a break from music and restoring a barn in Cornwall with his partner Fiona.

MURRAY, Anne

Singer songwriter and one time physical education teacher who became the first Canadian to win an American Gold disc (for Snowbird) . Despite international success as a singer, Murray has earned more respect for her charity work and in 1975 Queen Elizabeth bestowed upon her the highest honour possible for a Canadian citizen – Officer of the Order of Canada.

MURRAY, Ruby

A Fifties superstar who spent over 100 weeks in the charts of the time and unwittingly gave her name to the language of Cockney rhyming slang – Ruby Murray/Curry) and gave Nick Berry a 1992 chart success with a version of her first success, Heartbeat. Murray died on 17th December 1996 in Torbay aged 61 – she suffered liver failure as result of drink problems.

MUSICAL YOUTH

Formed by Freddy Waite and included his two sons Patrick and Junior, two brothers Kevin & Michael Grant and singer Dennis Seaton; the oldest was only 15 at the time of

Musical Youth

their No. 1 Pass The Dutchie. Seaton became a receptionist for a Birmingham Car Hire firm Michael does production work for Motown. Partick had a nervous breakdown and was convicted of joyriding at the age of 19, serving 12 months for drugs and theft. Three years later he served four years for assault and robbery then sadly died in 1993 when he fell and hit his head at a friends home. Dennis Seaton, the singer and songwriter, now fronts XMY (ex-Musical Youth) and is involved in charity fund raising; for whom he ran London Marathon.

NASH, Johnny

Probably best remembered for his 1972 hit I Can See Clearly Now but it was his Tears On My Pillow three years later that actually topped the charts. Although born in Texas, his influences were predominantly Caribbean reggae and he has now set up his own recording studio in the West Indies where he spends much of his time.

NASHVILLE TEENS

Original singer Ray Phillips had a spell with The Yardbirds Experience which was put together by Jim McCarty. He now fronts a new Nashville Teens to capitalise on the earlier success of their Tobacco Road. Away from the glitz of showbusiness he enjoys the glamour of Grand Prix motor racing and is employed by the McLaren racing team at their base in Weybridge, Surrey.
Tobacco Road (1964).

NAZARETH

Founder members Darrell Sweet, Dan McCafferty and Pete Agnew are still going strong on the Seventies rock circuit. Manny Charlton, the fourth original member, has since gone solo and moved into production and is re-locating to America. His place has been taken by former Stone The Crows keyboard player Ronnie Leahy. Short lived member Billy Rankin briefly joined a reformed Spiders From Mars and is now playing solo in Glasgow bars. Zal Cleminson has gone into computers.
This Flight Tonight (1973).

NELSON, Rick

Set out on his own solo career at the age of 16 and a year later chalked up his first success

with the million-selling A Teenager's Romance. Hello Mary Lou established him as a star and during the latter part of the Seventies he took part in numerous sessions but failed to achieve the success of his earlier career. Nelson died in 1985 when the charter plane carrying him between concert dates caught fire and crashed near De Kalb, Texas.

NELSON, Sandy

The first drummer to achieve solo success, scoring 1960's hits like 'Let There be Drums'. He provided inspiration for the likes of Cozy Powell who followed his lead a decade later. Following a motorcycle accident Nelson has his right foot and part of his leg amputated. 1982 but still managed to play regularly around Los Angeles and to record on his own label Veebltromics.

NEW KIDS ON THE BLOCK

New Kids on the Block burst onto the scene in 1989/90. In 1993 the group shortened their name to NKOTB and featured on the sound-track of the Free Willy movie. Two years later a US judge ruled that some profits made by the band should be paid to alleged Mafia member James Martorano who originally provided a $60,000 loan to help get the band started. The boys split shortly after.

Jordan Knight (singer) produced his own solo album; Donnie Wahlberg (brother of rapper/actor Marky Mark) and Danny Wood (both singers) also became producers. Joe MacKintyre made his acting debut in the movie version of The Fantastiks, while Jonathan Knight quit the music business altogether.

NEW SEEKERS

Rocketed to success shortly after their

formation in 1969 with a string of memorable chart hits. Original members Marty Kristian and Paul Layton are still touring under the band's name. This new version includes Mick Flynn who was previously in The Mixtures, the Australian band who had a massive hit with The Pushbike Song in the early Seventies. The Seekers fragmented in 1978. Lyn Paul has made a living from cabaret work and is currently appearing on stage in the touring version of Blood Brothers. Eve Graham left in 1978 with Danny Finn and they teamed up as a duo, touring together until 1985. She is now a solo performer and has recorded numerous jingles for corporate advertising campaigns.

I'd Like To Teach The World To Sing (1971).

NEW VAUDEVILLE BAND

Winchester Cathedral, their 1966 hit later went to the top of the American hit parade which prompted the group to move to Canada where they were based for the next three years. Grammy and Ivor Novello award winner Geoff Stephens had written the hit and formed the group using session musicians. He discovered and managed Donovan and later produced The Drifters and Dana. He is currently writing a musical with Don Black called Everything Terrific – Help! Geoff is married, with two daughters and a son and lives in Hertfordshire.

NEW YORK DOLLS

Outrageous American rockers whose lead singer, Johnny Thunders, also founded The Heartbreakers. He died in 1991 amid suspicious circumstances in a cheap New Orleans hotel room. Drummer Billy Mercia had died exactly twenty years before; he was found dead in his bath following an overdose while touring the United Kingdom. Jerry Nolan died in 1992 suffering from meningitis. Despite these tragedies, the remaing band still put on their extravagant stage make up and clothing to entertain audiences world wide.

NEWMAN, Randy

In 1996 sang You've Got A Friend from the sound-track of Toy Story with co-vocalist Lyle Lovett and also featured on the latest film score of Tim Burton's James And The Giant Peach, as well as touring around America.

NEWTON-JOHN, Olivia

In 1992 her Back To Basics album was released looking back over a 21-year singing career. She was also planning a US tour when she discovered that she had breast cancer so she withdrew from the public eye to recover. Within two years Newton-John was fit and well once more and started performing again.

In 1995 she separated from her husband of 10 years and returned to the English charts in a duet with Cliff Richard from his musical extravaganza Heathcliffe.

Nowadays much of her time is taken up caring for her 10 year old daughter and her work for the environment. She is spokesperson for The Children's Health and Environment Coalition (CHCE). As a sideline, she launched her own skin care line called Marae, made from seaweed.

Religion

Ten who have had the calling

1 Pat Boone
   Became presenter on Christian TV

2 RUN DMC
   Unlikely born again Christians

3 Sinitta
   Regular at Christian Life Centre

4 Al Green
   Now Rev. Al Green of The Full Gospel Tabernacle

5 Little Richard
   Seventh Day Adventist

6 Hank Marvin (Shadows) & Dave Hill (Slade)
   Jehovahs Witnesses

7 Joe Tex
   Spiritual Lecturer in Muslim faith, now also known as Yusef Hazziez

8 Barry McGuire
   Christian Evangelist

9 Millie
   Spreading God's gospel

10 Cat Stevens
   Moslem covert now called Yusef Islam

NICHOLAS, Paul

One time member of Screaming Lord Sutch's backing band who branched out from a successful stage acting career to play the part of pop star in the mid Seventies releasing four singles, two of which earned top ten placings. Has since returned to the theatre as performer and producer. 1997 sees him star in his first West End role in anything other than a musical.
Grandma's Party (1976).

NICHOLLS, Sue

Daughter of Lord Harmar-Nicholls the former Conservative MP, the Honourable Susan Harmar Nicholls (alias Audrey on Coronation Street) is perhaps best known for her role in Leonard Rossiter's Reggie Perrin series. Her 1968 hit Where Will You Be was ironically taken from the Street's early soap competitor Crossroads.

NILSSON

It was as a songwriter that Harry Nilsson first made a name for himself, but it was with the all time classic Without You (written by British songwriters Peter Ham & Tom Evans) that he topped the British and American Hit Parades in 1972. In 1994, having suffered a heart attack the previous year, Nilsson died in his sleep at his Agoura Hills home.
Without You (1972).

NIRVANA

Rebellious trio from Seattle. Since Kurt Cobain's death from a self inflicted gunshot wound on April 5th 1994, the group's drummer Dave Grohl has found more success with the Foo Fighters. Krist Novoselin (bass) now fronts his own band called Sweet 75.

NOONE, Peter

See HERMANS HERMITS.

NUMAN, Gary

Are Friends Electric and Cars dominated the UK charts in 1979. Numan later acquired his pilots license, spent a fortune on renovating his Harvard aeroplane and flew around the world. On one occasion, having endured a forced landing in India, was arrested for spying! He is now an internationally known aerobatics flyer. Former bass player Paul Gardiner died from a heroin overdose in 1984.

Paul Nicholas

Nirvana

Billy Ocean

OCEAN, Billy

Gentle disco and dance hits of the late Seventies and early Eighties set Billy Ocean up as a much in demand cabaret performer today.

Love Really Hurts Without You (1976).

O'CONNOR, Hazel

Soared to overnight success in the early Eighties when she starred in the rock film Breaking Glass. She then had a major hit with the

Hazel O'Connor

haunting Eighth Day in 1980. Despite the change in musical tastes with the flow of time, she has battled on undeterred and, apart from the occasional UK gig has worked extensively in Europe. She has also reorganised her personal life an lives in the relative tranquillity of Ireland.

Odyssey

ODYSSEY

Larger than life American duo who had their first chart success in 1977 with Native New Yorker. Recording together stopped in the late Eighties but they are still both involved in music.

Going Back To My Roots (1981).

O'FARIM, Esther and Abi

Husband and wife whose 1968 No. 1 Cinderella Rockerfella brought them brief international fame. Having returned home to Israel, the partnership and marriage broke up.

OLDFIELD, Mike

The 16 million seller Tubular

Mike Oldfield

Roy Orbison

Bells' was not just the start of Oldfield's career it was also the launching pad for Richard Branson's Virgin empire. Now with total album sales in excess of 40 million, Oldfield has moved to the Mediterranean to live in his newly built home on Ibiza.

ORBISON, Roy

Big O wrote Claudette (named after his wife who was later tragically killed in a motorbike accident) for the Everly Brothers. Only The Lonely, Running Scared and Cryin' were the earliest of his hits in a creer spanning over thirty years. He died in 1988.

Orbison had also been a member of the Travelling Wilburys and in 1992 his single I Drove All Night charted again as did Crying, a song that he had sung as a duet with k d Lang five years previously.
Oh Pretty Woman (1964).

O

ORLANDO, Tony

See DAWN.

OSMOND, Donny

See The OSMONDS.

OSMOND, Little Jimmy

In 1972 it would have been impossible to imagine that the Long Haired Lover From Liverpool would eventually become the rich saviour of the Osmond dynasty. Twenty five years on, Little Jimmy has established himself as an astute businessman with sufficient wealth to buy back much of the family empire that had been sold through their declining years. His entrepreneurial skills have flourished as a music business promoter. Also a blue belt in kung fu, his ability to speak fluent Japanese has meant that he has become a key figure in arranging tours to the Orient for a host of stars including the artist once known as Prince.

OSMOND, Marie

See The OSMONDS.

OSMONDS

Alan Osmond, an original member of the Seventies troupe, has eight sons who also perform and are known as The Osmonds – The Second Generation. His current hobby is raising ostriches at his Zion View Ostrich Farm. Alan was responsible for a lot of the group's special effects and is currently fascinated with fireworks.

Jay Osmond, the youngest of the original Osmond Brothers Quartet broke away from showbusiness to pursue an education at Brigham Young University in Utah. In 1993 he re-joined his brothers in Branson, Missouri at the Osmond Family Theatre and performs two shows a day six days a week. At the end of 1994 he released his own album It's About Time and later teamed up with Donny to co-producea CD and video compilation The Very Best of the Osmonds.

In 1978 Marie starred with Donny in a film called Going Coconuts and in the Eighties she returned to her first love which was recording country music. She has four children and released a video called Exercises For Mothers To Be as well as creating and manufacturing her own line of fine porcelain collector dolls. She spent a year and a half starring in the National Touring Company's version of The Sound of Music' throughout America performing the role of Maria.

Merrill was the lead singer on most of the Osmond's hits and after producing the Donny and Marie Show, he went on to produce films, television movies and TV specials. He claims to love fishing, hunting, camping, archery and back-packing. He is married to Mary and they have six children. He is also a talented artist and loves to paint whenever he can find the time.

Wayne Osmond was diagnosed as having cancer in 1996 and almost died. Trading on his nickname of Crazy Wayne, he has put together a number of joke books.

Donny is a qualified electrical engineer and supervised the wiring of the Osmond's huge production studio in Utah and then began his career come-back as a singer in the mid Eighties. He also gave up a promising racing career to take a gamble by accepting the lead role in Joseph & The Amazing Technicolour Dreamcoa opening in Toronto and has continued to perform in various cities

Gilbert O'Sullivan

OTIS, Johnny

Fifties crooner who had success with Ma, He's Making Eyes At Me. He opened the Johnny Otis Market and Deli in Saskatewen in 1990 and he performs regularly in the market's nightclub at the weekends.

PAPER DOLLS

British female trio discovered by a young Peter Stringfellow whose Something Here In My Heart in 1968 provided their solitary chart success. They carried on performing until 1979 when Susie Matthews, who was then known as Tiger, became a television and radio presenter in the North West, winning the Regional Presenter Of The Year award for her show on Manchester's Picadilly Radio.

Paper Lace

since. His stay in Chicago lasted a record breaking 16 months. He has also hosted shows for Satellite channel VH1.
Crazy Horses (1972).

O'SULLIVAN, Gilbert

Born in Co. Waterford, Ireland. He claims his early look was based on Charlie Chaplin and Buster Keaton; dressed in a flannel suit which was far too small, cropped punchball hair, flat cap, knee-length trousers and waistcoat. In 1972 he changed the style to collegiate monogrammed sweater and a longer hairstyle. Alone Again Naturally sold over 2 million copies in American alone and was No. 1 there for 6 weeks.

Gilbert O'Sullivan did not release any material in the 1980s due to a long-running litigation battle with his former manager, but in 1990 he wrote an autobiographical play called Every Song Has Its Play which was staged in England. Today he lives with his wife and two children on the Channel Islands in Jersey but has not stopped writing, spending days holed in a room in the house writing songs.

PAPER LACE

Made pop history in 1974 when their single The Night Chicago Died topped the American Hit Parade and later sold over a million copes. They were formed in Rochdale in 1968 and made a name for themselves on the TV talent show Opportunity Knocks. In 1974 Carlo Santanna left the group to go solo, though as yet, he has failed to make any major impact. Paper Lace, on the other hand, have continued to entertain. They even teamed up with Nottingham Forest Football Club to record the single We've Got The Whole World In Our Hands. They split in 1980 but re-formed three years later with a different line up. Their current set includes a Billy Fury medley as a tribute to the man that they backed for many years. Chris Raynor is the only surviving member from the Seventies.
Billy Don't Be A Hero (1974).

PARTRIDGE, Don

A remarkable story of a busker from Bournemouth who was spotted playing on the streets of London. He recorded two massive selling singles – Rosie and Blue Eyes – in 1968 and kept the press happy with a string of outrageous comments. He then returned to busking as if nothing had ever happened and is still entertaining passers-by some 25 years later.

PARTRIDGE FAMILY

Sprung from the popular Seventies television series of the same name. Since the end of its run in 1974 the leading members have gone in various directions.

Susan Dey did some television work after The Partridge Family and became a big star through the series LA Law. Dey is now a member of the Advisory Council for Violence Against Women in America and is still in demand as an actress both in film and on TV. She made her debut as a film producer on I Love You Perfect.

Danny Bonaduce has been the subject of many tabloid newspaper stories during the last few years. After his arrest for reportedly beating up a transvestite prostitute in 1990, he began to clean up his act and went on the road as a comedian. He even toured as David's opening act for many dates on his 1990 come-back tour. Currently Danny is a DJ at WLUP FM in Chicago where he lives with his wife, Gretchen.

Dave Madden has been doing voice-over commercial work for many years and Tracy runs a bookstore in Temecula.

As for the two actors who played Chris; Jeremy Gelbwaks lives in New Orleans working as a computer analyst; Brian Forstur, is a racing car driver and instructor in California.

Shirley Jones makes few television appearances today but occasionally she appears in summer season theatre productions.
Breaking Up Is Hard To Do (1972).

PAT and MICK

Their popularity as Capital Radio disc jockeys helped Pat Sharp and Mick Brown. Brown is still with the station while Sharp left after nine years to work on TV. He now hosts the Breakfast show on Liberty Radio and presents the ITV kids show Funhouse.
I Haven't Stopped Dancing Yet (1989).

PAUL, Owen

Brother of Simple Minds drummer Brian McGee who became a producer before moving to America to teach at the College of Performing Arts in Florida. He returned to England in 1991 with his wife and three children. and now concentrates on TV and Show music.
Favourite Waste Of Time (1986).

PARTON, David

Discovered Sweet Sensation and co-wrote their number one hit Sad Sweet Dreamer with Tony Hatch. Managed a solo hit in 1977 with his version of Stevie Wonder's Isn't She Lovely. Now a producer but still writing, from his base in Stoke On Trent.

PAYNE, Freda

After her 1970 chart-topper Band Of Gold Payne returned to her jazz and classical roots. In the Nineties she diversified into television and presented her own show in America – For You Black Woman.

PEACHES & HERB

The original soul singing duo were Francine Hurd – nicknamed Peaches – and Herb Feenster who retired in 1970. Returning to their home town of Washington, Peaches became a housewife and Herb went into Law Enforcement. In 1978 Herb linked up with a new Peaches and decided to try again. Within two years they scored their biggest hit – Reunited. In 1981 they were the first black entertainers to perform in China. Feenster continues to play under the name in the supper clubs of America.

PEPSI AND SHIRLIE

Former backing singers for Wham who scored two top ten hits of their own in the Eighties. Both singers have since separately been declared bankrupt due to unpaid tax. Pepsi had been appearing in West End shows while Shirlie is now married to Martin Kemp (Spandau Ballet).
Heartache (1987).

PERKINS, Carl

Perkins wrote and recorded the Fifties classic

Authors

Ten who have put pen to paper

1 Joe Brown *Brown Sauce*
2 Nick Van Eade *Cutting Crew*
3 Brian Poole *Talk Back*
4 Ian Gillan *Poetry*
5 Labi Siffre *Poetry*
6 George Harrison
7 Sean Mayes *Tom Robinson Band*
8 Laurie Anderson *Various Novels*
9 Pat Boone *Religious Books*
10 Cheryl Baker *Cook Book*

Blue Suede Shoes long before Elvis Presley made it his own. In March 1956 a car accident killed his brother Jay and his manager, and put Carl in hospital for a year with a broken neck and fractured skull. When he finally recovered, he never quite managed to replicate his early success. Carl Perkins is still touring in his own right, albeit as a country artist, and has also established the Carl Perkins Centre for the Prevention of Child Abuse.
Blue Suede Shoes (1956).

PETER & GORDON

Peter Asher, brother of actress Jane, and Gordon Waller were old school friends. Their A World Without Love was No. 1 in England in 1964 and True Love Ways reached No. 2 the following year. In 1967 they split as a full-time act although they continued to occasionally record together, finally splitting in 1968. Asher became A&R Manager at the Beatles' Apple Records before developing his career as a manager and producer, initially at MGM Records in Los Angeles. Asher moved to Malibu and picked up a Producer of the Year Award in 1990. He is still producing and managing acts today, including 10,000 Maniacs and Randy Newman.

Waller moved into acting and was cast as Pharaoh in the London production of Tim Rice and Andrew Lloyd-Webber's Joseph And The Amazing Technicolour Dreamcoat in the seventies then he retired from the music scene. After a spell as a Rank Xerox salesman he moved to Fowey in Cornwall in 1987 to run a gift store and dinghy repair shop. He was cleared of sending an indecent fax message by Bodmin Magistrates Court in Cornwall on April 4th 1992.

PETER, PAUL, & MARY

Mary Travers, Peter Yarrow and Paul Stookey. had hits with Puff the Magic Dragon and If I Had A Hammer in the Sixties. They were also regular attendees at protest rallies during the Vietnam era. They recorded John Denver's Leaving on a Jet Plane in 1970 and sold a million copies.

The following year they decided that they had had enough and split to go solo. Just after the band were awarded a Grammy Award for Best Children's Record of the Year Peter Yarrow was jailed for three months after being found guilty of a sex offence – 'taking immoral liberties with a 14 year old girl' – of which he was vindicated ten years later. He returned to music as a session musician and wrote Mary MacGregor's huge hit in 1977 Torn Between Two Lovers.

Mary Travers went into radio and television work as an interviewer and had her own chat show, while Paul Stookey returned to his folk roots, working in his self-built studio and performing in folk clubs.

They got back together again and in 1995 Peter, Paul and Mary released a new album called Lifelines on Warner Brothers.
Leaving On A Jet Plane (1970).

PICKETT, Wilson

In 1965 he co-wrote and recorded the million-selling souls classic In The Midnight Hour. In 1974 he was arrested in possession of a gun and had had numerous run-ins with the law, largely as a result of excessive drinking. He was arrested in 1992 for striking an 86 year old and in 1993 was sentenced to one year in jail for a drinking offence and had to undergo treatment for alcoholism. HE came out of jail on five year's probation but was arrested again at his New Jersey home and charged with possession of two grams of cocaine. Despite all this, Wilson Pickett performs regularly and is very active on the recording scene.

PILOT

Formed by two ex-Bay City Rollers, Billy Lyall and David Paton. After a short chart run

which included top ten's January and Magic, the band went their separate ways. Billy Lyall briefly joined a version of Dollar but died in 1989. He was only five stone at the time, his body having been decimated by AIDs. Original member Stuart Tosh joined 10cc in 1976; David Paton and Ian Bairson became session musicians and Paton has also co-written with Fish and played with Elton John's band.

Pink Floyd now and then (above)

PINK FLOYD

Original member Syd Barrett developed adrugs problem and was asked to leave the group in 1968. He returned to Cambridge where he lived in isolation and is now rumoured to have taken up painting. In 1979 the band suffered financial problems when Norton Warburg, who handled their business affairs, collapsed. Diverifying into film to accompany there ever more elaborate stage shows, The Wall opened in 1982 with Bob Geldof appearing in a leading role.

Rick Wright has homes in London and the south of France where he lives with former model wife Millie. Nick Mason is regularly seen at Race meetings and has a collection of Ferraris and aeroplanes. One time collaborator and writer (Atom Heart Mother) Ron Geesin is now working on 'interactive art' with occasional TV work and the odd solo album.

Another Brick In The Wall (1979).

PITNEY, Gene

Invested his earnings from music wisely and can boast ownership of a beach and yacht club where, in poorer days, he worked as a chef. He also takes an active role in his publishing operation which includes three separate music and production companies. In

1989 he had a UK No. 1 with Marc Almond, formerly of Soft Cell, with his old hit Something's Gotten Hold Of My Heart and is today still a popular live draw in America. Pitney lives in Connecticut with his wife Lynne and three sons.
Twenty Four Hours From Tulsa (1963).

PLATTERS

Despite the death of many of the original members, the Platters name lives on through an ensemble put together by the band's original business manager Gene Bennett. Paul Orobi died in 1989 at the age of 58. David Lynch died of cancer on January 2nd 1981. Nate Nelson died on June 1st 1984, also of cancer. Tony Williams, the original lead vocalist, died in his sleep at his Manhattan penthouse suffering from diabetes and emphysema in 1982. In 1995, Orobi's widow won the latest round to recover royalty rights due fromThe Platter's recordings.
Only You (1956).

POLICE

In 1995 Sting's accountant was jailed for six years having been found guilty of stealing a staggering £6million from the singer.

Drummer Stuart Copeland is now recognised as a leading writer and performer in screen sound track production and has worked on numerous television programmes, including Wall Street and Highlander II. He also composes for opera, symphony and ballet companies across America. Sting combines a solo career with his active interest in the environment

POOLE, Brian

Was the Tremeloes' frontman for hits including Twist And Shout and their 1963 No.1 Do You Love Me. After a spell out of the business following his split from the Trems in

Brian Poole of the Tremeloes now and then (below)

1966, Poole returned to music and is now performing regularly with his new backing band The Electrix.

His daughters Chelle & Karen have followed in fathers footsteps achieving chart success as Alisha's Attic. Now fluent in Back Slang, he has recently had book about the English Language published by Avon Books called Talk Back.

THE POPPY FAMILY

Consisted of Terry Jacks and his first wife, Susan. While Terry became world famous thanks to his Seventies hit Seasons In The Sun, Susan is now in Nashville doing commercials.
Which Way You Goin' Billy (1970).

POWELL, Cozy

Made his name with Jeff Beck and a clutch of drum based solo hits in the Seventies such as Dance With The Devil (No. 3 in 1973). He has been in regular demand since performing with Rainbow, Whitesnake, Black Sabbath and ELP. He recently toured with ex-Fleetwood Mac guitarist Peter Green as part of his Splinter Group and also with the Brian May band.

PRESLEY, Elvis

In August 1977 the King collapsed and died – he was just 42. Twenty years on he is still his record company's best selling artist. His former home Graceland is visited by over 750,000 people each year making it second only to the White House as the most popular attraction. There is a multi-million pound reward for anyone who can find Elvis alive – so far there have been over 250,000 alleged sightings!

PRESTON, Billy

As well as performing as a solo singer and organist, Preston has worked with many artists from the Beatles to Stevie Wonder's wife Syreeta (with whom he had his biggest UK success With You I'm Born Again). He was arrested in 1991 on drugs charges and ordered to join a re-hab centre , remaining in demand as a session musician ever since.

PRESTON, Johnny

Fifties vocalist Preston retired from showbusiness in 1962, only two years after

Johnny Preston

Running Bear had brought him a U No. 1 and made him an international star. However, the lure of cabaret dollars lured him back to earn more churning out old hits

PRETTY THINGS

Phil May (lead vocalist) quits in 1969 to become a producer. The band re-formed briefly in the Seventies and then again in the next decade to work part-time working the pubs and clubs and they continue to perform selected dates during today, although they are still banned from New Zealand!

Phil May married an aristocrat and attended Charles and Di's wedding but remains a true rock n roller. Dick Allen, who left the Rolling Stones when they turned pro, is the only other original member still involved and lives a quiet life on Isle Of Wight.
Don't Bring Me Down (1964).

PRICE, Alan

see THE ANIMALS.

PROBY, P J

Born in Houston, Texas. Made his name in the early Sixties sporting flamboyant clothes and in 1964 had to be hauled off stage by theatre management when his skin tight velvert trousers burst open. This prompted a ban from appearing in theatres throughout the country but boosted his profile considerably. In 1967 he filed for bankruptcy in Los Angeles and in the following year was also made bankrupt in England but then fled back to America reputedly to breed horses. In 1977, starred as Elvis Presley in the rock musical Elvis in London's West End.

In 1991 he suffered a heart attack whilst living in a terraced house in Bolton. More recently he has pulled both his trousers and his act together and starred with the Who in Quadrophenia on stage and released an unlikely duet with Marc Almond. Nowadays staying out of trouble, he is reportedly tee-total and living alone in a rented flat in Barnet.

Hold Me (1964).

PROCOL HARUM

Their standard, A Whiter Shade of Pale, sold more than ten million copies and topped the charts in 1967. The band split up completely ten years later. Dave Knights left to pursue a career in management. Matthew Fisher, keyboard player, also left to go into production. Robin Trower started a solo career. Gary Brooker, lead vocalist and pianist, went on to join Eric Clapton's backing band in the late Eighties and then turned his hand to writing ballet scores.

PJ Proby now

Procul Harum

They re-formed in 1991 and in 1996 following a successful American tour they returned home to play their first live shows in over a decade and even teamed up with the London Symphony Orchestra to play at the Barbican to coincide with the release of a Best Of album. Brooker appeared in the film version of Evita playing Juan Peron's Foreign Minister and also has fun in his R & B band, No Stiletto Shoes which also features Andy Fairweather-Low (see Amen Corner). He also found time to play with Ringo Star's All Stars in 1997.

Whiter Shade Of Pale (1967).

PROTHEROE, Brian

A Shakespearean actor who joined the select band of one hit wonders in 1974 with Pinball. Has since starred on our television screens in Gentlemen and Players and in Granada TV's adaptation of a Jeffery Archer novel.

PUCKETT, Gary & The Union Gap

Young Girl topped both the British and American charts in 1968 but the boom faded as quickly as it had arrived. Puckett turned to acting and created a second lucrative career in films, television and theatre.

PYTHON LEE JACKSON

Rod Stewart's (recorded pre-Maggie May) uncredited vocals made a name for this unknown group in 1972. Stewart's fee reportedly paid for a new set of stretch covers for his car seats!

In A Broken Dream (1972).

QUATRO, Suzi

Once a leather-clad rocker whose worldwide record sales now exceed 45 million with 16 hit singles and 25 years performing in concert. Quatro has forged a successful career in TV since her Seventies heyday, starting with the cult TV programme Happy Days.

In 1982 she became hostess of the UK day-time programme Gas Street and remained a TV personality throughout the Eighties. Stage roles beckoned in 1991 and she appeared in the musical Tallulah Who which she co-wrote with Willie Russell following a nine month run in the London's West End in Annie Get Your Gun.

Suzi Quatro

She is married to German promoter Reiner Haas and still performing occasional live date, splitting her time between homes in Hamburg and Essex.

Her former husband Len Tuckey, who she divorced in 1992, is now manager of Slade II.
Can The Can (1973).

QUEEN

Brian May, Roger Taylor, John Deacon and Freddie Mercury were all college students and established Queen as one of the foremost international acts of all time. Lead singer Mercury died in November 1991. The remaining three still play together as well as pursuing their individual musical interests.

RAFFERTY, Gerry

After singing with Stealer's Wheel he had a huge success with Baker Street in 1978 as a solo performer. In the early Eighties he travelled with his family and spent a year in Italy before driving across North America. Now involved in music only accasionally, he produced the Proclaimer's No. 3 hit Letter From America.
Baker Street (1978).

Gerry Rafferty

RAINBOW

see DEEP PURPLE.

RANKIN DREAD

Hey Fatty Boom Boom was an instantly recognisable hit in 1980 however Rankin Dread (also known as Errol Codling, real name Robert Blackwood, and a string of aliases) was deported from England in 1988 being branded the 'most dangerous foreign national in Britain', believed to be a leading Jamaican Yardie gangster.

RAY, Johnny

Wrote his first million seller, Little White

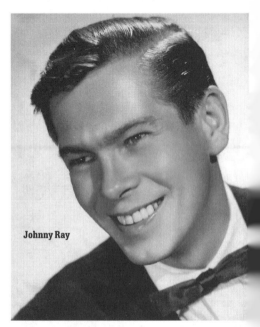
Johnny Ray

Cloud, at the age of seventeen and had further hits with Just Walkin In The Rain and I'll Never Fall in Love Again. He achieved success despite having to rely on a hearing aid. The charity to help the deaf, HEAR, christened him their 'singing disciple'. He died in Los Angeles on 24th February 1990.
Just Walkin In The Rain (1956).

Amoo of Real Thing (right)

REAL THING

In the Seventies, the growth of disco soul and its prominence in the British pop charts was epitomised by Liverpudlian childhood pals the Real Thing – brothers Eddy and Chris Amoo won TV talent show Opportunity Knocks in 1972. Since the Eighties the band have been out of the limelight in terms of recording but have maintained a busy agenda on the performing front. Chris and his wife have taken a serious interest in dog breeding and achieved a major success when their Afghan hound Gable won the cherished Pup Of The Year award and later the Supreme Champion Award at the famous Crufts Dog Show. Chris became the first pop personality ever to win this award. Chris and Eddy have now developed their own 16 track studio.
You To Me Are Everything (1976).

REDDING, Otis

The Sixties soul star was killed on December 10th, 1967 when his plane crashed in heavy fog into the frozen Lake Monana, near Madison, Wisconsin, to where he and his group were travelling for an engagement – he was only 26. Four members of The Bar Keys died with him. At his funeral in Macon City, 4,500 people turned up for the memorial service, including many of the world's top soul artists. Not long afterwards, Sitting On The Dock Of The Bay topped the American chart.
Fa Fa Fa Fa Fa (Sad Song) (1967).

REDDY, Helen

After a hit with Angie Baby in 1975 she appeared as the singing nun in the movie Airport 75 and has continued to act in films like Pete's Dragon and Sergeant Pepper's Lonely Hearts Club Band with the Bee Gees. She made a switch to jazz-orientated material in the latter part of the Eighties and has toured with Mel Torme as well as a variety of other jazz artists. She has also taken stage roles in West End musicals.

REEVES, Jim

Former disc jockey and baseball player Reeves died in a plane crash in 1964, however the success of his ballads thereafter must have been the envy of many artists of the time. In September 1964 eight out of the top 20 albums in the charts were his.
Distant Drums (1976).

Jim Reeves

REEVES, Martha
See MARTHA & VANDELLAS.

REFLEX
Paul Fishman was on keyboards and now writes and produces for the likes of Yazz as well as writing the music score for two ballets. Roland Kerridge appeared in Gilbert O'Sullivan's backing group and became a presenter on MTV before being reduced to producing the traffic news on local radio.
The Politics Of Dancing (1984).

REID, Neil
Won Opportunity Knocks with Mother Of Mine at the age of 12. Other than a brief unsuccessful comeback Reid has kept away from the music business. He worked in catering before finding work as an insurance salesman. Now in his mid-thirties, he lives in Blackpool.
Mother Of Mine (1972).

Cliff Richard

RICH, Charlie
Accomplished country singer who broke into the pop charts in 1974 with The Most Beautiful Girl and Behind Closed Doors in 1974. Rich died of a blood clot in his lungs at the age of 62 in July 1995.

RICHARD, Cliff
Sir Cliff is the Peter Pan of pop and has maintained a loyal fan following over a career spanning almost four decades and more chart hits than any other artist.

RIGHTEOUS BROTHERS
Bill Medley and Bobby Hatfield parted company in 1968 to pursue solo careers. They re-formed in 1974 and enjoyed two more hits then returned to the process of carving out their own careers as individuals.

In 1987 Bill Medley and Jennifer Warnes performed a duet in the movie Dirty Dancing and had a hit I Had The Time Of My Life in the same year. The following year he had a hit with his version of the Hollies' song He Ain't Heavy, He's My Brother taken from the soundtrack of the Rambo III film.

Then in 1990 The Righteous Brothers' Unchained Melody was used in the film Ghost and gave them an unexpected No. 1.
'You've Lost That Lovin' Feeling (1965).

RILEY, Jeannie C
After selling over four million copies of the 1968 hit Harper Valley PTA, Jeannie Riley turned to singing in nightclubs, but later decided to concentrate on concerts. She lives in Brentwood, Tennessee with her daughter Kim, and averages fifteen to twenty concert appearances each month.

RIPERTON, Minnie
Soft voiced Riperton had a hit with Loving You in the spring of 1975 on both sides of the Atlantic. She died on July 12, 1979 after undergoing three years of cancer therapy.

ROBBINS, Marty
One of Nashville's leading stars whose biggest UK hit was with Devil Woman in 1962. Following years of heart trouble he died in Nashville in 1982.
El Paso (1960).

ROBINSON, Smokey & The Miracles

The Miracles still continue to appear in cabaret today. Ronnie White lost a fourteen month battle with leukaemia so did not live to join the reunion – they now perform with only three singers instead of four out of respect to him.
Tears Of A Clown (1970)

ROBINSON, Tom

Suffered a nervous breakdown at age of 16 and then spent six years in Finchden Manor for disturbed adolescents. Had success in the late Seventies as the Tom Robinson Band (TRB) then with Sector 27. He lived in Hamburg and had a setback when the band's management company went bankrupt.

Returning to the UK, he built a home studio,

Tom Robinson

presented BBC Radio 4 series The Locker Room and most recently contributed to a Multi Media CD-Rom and released a new album in 1996. In November 96 he received an Honorary Master Of Arts Degree from the University of Teesside. Robinson discovered bi-sexuality and became a father at the age of 40. Keyboard player and author Sean Mayes died of AIDs at the age of 49. – he had written biographies about Kate Bush and Joan Armatrading.
2-4-6-8 Motorway (1977).

ROCKIN BERRIES

Now 35 years since their first top ten hit with He's In Town back in the Sixties. In the Nineties they were voted one of the best Cabaret Acts in the UK. for their own combination of comedy and music which keeps them very much in demand for theatres, clubs and corporate work.
Poor Mans Son (1965).

Rockin Berries now

RODGERS, Clodagh

Country singer from Ireland who made a comeback in 1996 starring as Mrs Johnstone in the touring version of Blood Brothers.

RODGERS, Jimmy

Best known for his top five success English Country Garden, released in 1962. In 1967 he was involved in a car accident in Los Angeles when he was found in his own car with a fractured skull; he could recall nothing about the incident. However, during the following year he underwent major brain surgery and it was touch and go whether he would ever recover. Jimmy eventually became an active evangelist living in Los Angeles.

ROE, Tommy

Had a No. 1 success with Dizzy in 1969. The Seventies saw him as a major nightclub attraction, a position he has retained ever since. Twice-married, Roe still has two homes – one in his native Atlanta and the other in Los Angeles. He drifted from public view apart from the occasional entry in the country music charts. However, his hit Dizzy was re-

Bill Wyman's Sticky Fingers restaurant

worked by Vic Reeves and the Wonderstuff and topped the UK charts in 1991.

ROLLING STONES

Originally a six-piece band but pianist Ian Stewart became their road manager – he died from a heart attack in 1985 whilst in the waiting room of his doctor's surgery. The second guitarist was Dick Taylor, a friend of Jagger and Richard at Sidcup Art School, and he left early on to form Pretty Things. Brian Jones drowned in his swimming pool in 1969 and was replaced by Mick Taylor who left the band in 1974. Former Faces guitarist Ron Wood took over and has been a permanent member of the band since 1978, still performing with Jagger and Richards. Bill Wyman has now left the band to follow solo interests.

RONETTES

Veronica Bennett, Estelle Bennett and Nedra Talley (two sisters and their cousin) – three New York Puerto Rican girls – became the Ronettes in 1959. After a handful of hits they faded into obscurity.

In 1968, Veronica (Ronnie) Bennett married the group's mentor Phil Spector although they later divorced. A year later, the group (minus their newly-married lead singer) made a brief comeback and Veronica has made numerous comeback attampts ever since. Going into the Nineties, Ronnie Bennett is an occasional performer at benefit

Breeding

Ten who have followed in the footsteps

1 Alishas Attic – Brian Poole
2 Natalie Cole – Nat King Cole
3 Sam Brown – Joe Brown
4 Kim Wilde – Marty Wilde
5 3T – Tito Jackson
6 Roseanne Cash – Johnny Cash
7 Debby Boone – Pat Boone
8 Zak Starkey – Ringo Starr
9 Julian Lennon – John Lennon
10 Chesney Hawkes – Chip Hawkes

Brian Ferry of
Roxy Music

concerts and nostalgia events and she has
recorded with Joey Ramone as well as hoping
to end a 10-year battle with ex-husband Phil
which would then allow her to
sing her greatest hits again.
Be My Baby (1963).

ROSE ROYCE

During the late Seventies
she earned 12 gold
records and five
platinum discs hits
such as Car Wash and
Wishing On A Star.
They currently tour
Europe three times a
year and Japan twice
a year. Former gospel choir singer Gwen
Dickey left in 1981 to pursue a solo career and
she returned to the UK charts with Chaka
Khan's Ain't Nobody.

ROSS, Diana

See The SUPREMES.

ROWLES, John

Singer from New Zealand remembered for his
1968 No. 3 If I Only Had Time, Rowles has
established himself as a big time entertainer
in his homeland and in Hawai i. He was
presented with Hawaii's greatest
entertainment honour – No Ka Oi – and in
1980 was awarded the OBE for services to
entertainment.

ROXY MUSIC

Created in 1971 by art student Bryan Ferry,
Brian Eno and Andy Mackay who were later
joined by Phil Manzanera who had been the
band's sound engineer. Eno left in 1973 and
has since become an innovative solo artist
and producer, having worked on albums by
U2 (including The Joshua Tree &

142

Unforgettable Fire) and David Bowie among many others. He is also now a visiting Professor at the Royal College of Art and a patron of the charity War Child.

Andy Mackay provided the music for the television series Rock Follies and teamed up with Phil Manzenera to form the Explorers with limited success. He also published a book called Electronic Music. Brian Ferry has continued to enjoy hige success as a solo artist.

Virginia Plain (1972).

Rubettes

RUBETTES

the flat-capped chaps hit the top of the charts with Sugar Baby Love, their very first single and the first of 15 international hits establishing them as one of the most successful bands of the Seventies. The band retired in 1981 when the various members pursued solo projects until being asked to tour Germany three years later. With three of the original members in attendance, namely Alan Williams, Mick Clarke and Bill Hurd, the Rubettes are still reproducing their nostalgic sound some fifteen years on. Alan Williams charted as The Firm with Arthur Daley (E's Alright) in 1982. Pete Armison, an American who left the band after only six months, worked with the Hollies in the Eighties and became a session musician based in Seattle. Tony Thorpe moved to Burnley where he plays jazz and blues in local music haunts and took up work as a journalist. John Richardson left showbiz in search of religion and is now a staunch devotee writing and producing Christian music. He has also been working for the past ten years as a homeopathic healer and masseur.

Juke Box Jive (1974).

RUNAWAYS

The Runaways were fronted by Cherie Currie, Lita Ford and Joan Jett. Jett went on to have solo success with I Love Rock n Roll and in 1995 Ford launched Lita Ford Bodywear, manufactured by Glamorous Appeal in Miami.

RUN DMC

Archetypal American bad boy rappers who showed the world how to Walk This Way in 1986. They have now discovered a new path of their own – as successful born again Christians. Run-Simmonds is now an ordained minister at his own ministry's church in Manhattan, New York and has released his first album on his new Gospel label, Rev Run Records. The group also still perform as a trio.

RYAN, Paul and Barry

Twin sons of Fifties singing star Marion Ryan and tour promoter Harold Davidson. The duo split in 1968 and Paul concentrated on songwriting and record production. Frank Sinatra had a major hit with the Paul Ryan song I Will Drink The Wine in 1971.

Barry Ryan reached No. 2 in Britain with Eloise (written by brother Paul). In 1976 he married Princess Meriam of Johore, daughter of the late Sultan of Johore, who was one of the richest men in the world. The marriage lasted for four years before ending in divorce in 1980. Barry still works on the club circuit.

Bobby Rydell

RYDELL, Bobby

After his singing career finished he has continued to perform on the nostalgia circuit and has the honour of having the school in the film Grease named after him.

Suicides

Ten who did 'emselves in

1   Peter Ham (Badfinger)
2   Danny Rapp (Danny & Juniors)
3   Singing Nun
4   Terry Kath (Chicago)
5   Marge Ganser (Shangri Las)
6   Del Shannon
7   Paul Williams (Temptations)
8. Faron Young
9   Tom Evans (Badfinger)
10 Richard Manuel (The Band)

SAILOR

Scored successive triumphs with A Glass Of Champagne and Girls, Girls, Girls in 1975/6. Phil Pickett (keyboards) joined Culture Club, wrote Karma Chameleon and the 1984 Olympic Games theme for ITV. Drummer Grant Serpell now works as a schoolteacher in Maidenhead, while George Kajanus, who claimed to be a Norwegian Prince, has written a piece for the Edinburgh Festival. Henry Marsh wrote a musical about surfing. The original quartet have been touring successfully since reuniting in 1991. Phil Pickett played medieval instruments (crumhom) on several Richard Thompson albums.

ST CECILIA

Encouraged us to Leap Up And Down (Wave Your Knickers In The Air) in 1971. Former DJ and band member Bip Wetherell now owns a night club, theme pub and recording studio, as well as performing with a reformed version of The Tornados. The group also tour the clubs with a show called Pop Goes The Sixties featuring archive news footage and slide production – even though they had their biggest hit in the Seventies!

ST PETERS, Crispian

Once claimed that he was the second Elvis and had more talent than all four Beatles combined. Tried his hand at country music however he suffered from stroke a few years ago effectively ending his career. Turns out very infrequently at local venues close to his home in Swanley in Kent.

St WINIFREDS School Choir

St Winifred's school in Stockport still has a choir so there is always a danger that there might be another hit in the vein of There's No -one Quite Like Grandma.

SAINTE-MARIE, Buffy

A folk singer/songwriter of Indian descent Sainte-Marie had written numerous hits for Glen Campbell, Bobby Darin, and even Elvis, before her own name appeared in the British chart of 1971 with Soldier Blue. She effectively retired to bring up a family and to devote more time to her charity interests but later won an Oscar for her composition Up Where We Belong for the film Officer And A Gentleman.

SAKAMOTO, Kyo

Japanese singer who had a world-wide hit with Sukiyaki in 1963 (a version by Kenny Ball also hit the top ten in the same year). Sakamoto died in 1985 when he was one of 524 passengers killed when a Boeing 747 crashed outside Tokyo.

SAM & DAVE

Sam Moore and Dave Prater's Soul Man only made 24 in the UK charts but was a million seller in the State and is now regarded as a soul classic. The duo split in 1970 to go their own separate ways but re-formed in 1971 to play rock and soul clubs all over the States. Interest in the duo was revitalised in 1979 with The Blues Brothers revival of Soul Man. In 1981 the partnership was permanently dissolved with Prater going on to tour with Sam Daniels as Sam and Dave the following year. In 1987 Prater was arrested for selling crack to an undercover cop and sentenced to three years probation. In 1988 he was killed when his car left the road and hit a tree near Syracuse. In 1995 Moore re-emerged at the Hall of Fame concert in Cleveland, Ohio.

SAM THE SHAM & The Pharoahs

His real name was Domingo Samudio but he's much better known as Sam the Sham. Their image consisted of wearing brightly-coloured

Arab clothes and in the early Seventies Sam tried to carve a solo career as Sam Samudio. He now works in record production.
Wooly Bully (1965).

SAMSON

Heavy Metal Rockers with a cult following. Paul Samson is still recording and touring although he is an electrician by day. Thunderstick (the wild drummer) recorded a solo album then had various jobs, including painting and decorating. Bruce Dickinson joined Iron Maiden, while Nicky Moore is still touring with his own blues band.

SANDPIPERS

In 1976 they had a hit with Hang on Sloopy, by which time the group had been together for over 16 years. The trio sing in eleven languages and continue to entertain cabaret audiences around the world.
Guantanamera (1966).

SARNE, Mike

Enjoyed his greatest chart success with two novelty songs in 1962, Step Outside and Will I What – the first being a duet with future Eastenders star Wendy Richard. Became a film maker and was responsible for the 1995 film The Punk & The Princess.

SARSTEDT, Peter

Guitarist who first came to prominence in 1969 with Where Do You Go To My Lovely which stayed at No. 1 for four weeks and was awarded the Ivor Novello Award for Best Song of 1969-70. After three years living in Denmark he returned to live with his mum in Croydon and became a travelling poet. Now lives in Coulsdon writing songs and touring with revival tour packages. Last year he announced that he has written a sequel to his chart-topper called Lovely Two!

SARSTEDT, Robin

Brother of Peter (see above) and also fellow Sixties star Eden Kane (Richard Sarstedt). Had a hit in 1976 with a revival of the Fifties song My Resistance Is Low. Robin is still a full time singer and happy touring small clubs.

SAVALAS, Telly

Appeared in numerous major films and made over 100 episodes of Kojak between 1973 and 1978. The lollipop sucker topped the charts in 1975 with his version of David Gates's If. Died in 1994 from prostate cancer.

SAVOY BROWN

One of the most influential British blues outfits were formed in 1965 and have since had over 64 members. The only original member being the founder, Kim Simmonds. Keyboard player Bob Hall now lives in Sheffield and has been instrumental in establishing the National Centre For Popular

Peter Sarstedt
then and now

Music based in the town. Leo Manning is now an offocer at the Inland Revenue. Ray Chappell now claims to be better known in mountain climbing circles. Martin Stone has run second hand bookshops for many years and now lives in Paris.

Leo Sayer

SAYER, Leo

Adopted the image of a sad clown and reached No. 1 in 1977 with When I Need You. In 1988 he embarked on a self-financed UK tour and his former manager Adam Faith paid him a reported £650,000 as settlement of owed earnings and record royalties. He wrote hits for Roger Daltrey (Giving It All Away) and then wrote his own The Show Must Go On and You Make Me Feel Like Dancing. Leo spent most of the Eighties writing and releasing product in Europe and in 1993 he resolved all his long-running financial differences with his former label Chrysalis, and the Leo Sayer Greatest Hits CD was released.

SAYLE, Alexei

Anarchic comedian Sayle has a multitude of talents, having appeared in Shakespeare at the Old Vic, on television, in films and co-writing The Young Ones. He has also presented a television documentary – The History Of The Ford Cortina – which could

have served as inspiration for his only chart entry.
Ullo John Got A New Motor? (1984).

SCAFFOLD

Liverpudlian group founded by Mike McGear (Paul McCartney's younger brother), Roger McGough and John Gorman. Lily The Pink and Thank U Very Much elevated them to cult status before their demise in 1974. McGear went on to write a children's book and bring up his three daughters after his wife of 13 years left in 1978. He has also had his photographic work exhibited in Liverpool. John Gorman achieved television notoriety presenting the popular children's programme Tiswas. Gorman now lives on a farm in France and occasionally appears in films. Roger McGough has since become best known for his poetry.

SEARCHERS

Tony Jackson, Chris Curtis, Mike Pender and John McNally were the founder members. Frank Allenand Billy Adamson joined in the late Sixties. They claim that they never made any money in theur heyday but are in demand and touring 52 weeks a year now. Chris Curtis (drummer) left in 1966 and now works in the health service. Mike Pender started his own version called Mike Pender Searchers in 1985. Tony Jackson who sang on the early hits left in 1964. He ran Rasputins club in Majorca for five years before taking over the management of a golf club. He made a return to live shows in the early Nineties but was involved in a violent incident in a Liverpool pub and imprisoned in Walton Jail.
Needles and Pins (1964).

SEEKERS

Keith Potger, Bruce Woodley, Athol Guy and Ken Ray were joined by Judith Durham on vocals. Their first single, I'll Never Find Another You, topped the British charts at the beginning of 1965 and was followed by a string of hits. They were one of the first Australian groups to succeed internationally and had hits with Morningtown Ride and Georgy Girl (from the film of the same name, which was co written by Jim Dale). In 1968 they disbanded.

Athol Guy made numerous appearances on radio and television before forming his own

Mike Pender of the Searchers now and the whole group then (above)

marketing and promotions company. Bruce Woodley returned home to Australia to successfully write music for TV and radio commercials.

Keith Potger remained in Britain to form The New Seekers and for a while appeared on stage with the group before concentrating on their management. Judith Durham stayed in Britain but returned to her jazz roots. The group re-formed for a 25th Anniversary Tour in 1993-4.

SELECTER
Pauline Black became an actress. Bassist Charlie Anderson moved to Kenya to become an hotel's entertainment manager. Harrington Bainbridge found employment as a Youth Justice worker in the Midlands, while Compton Ambrose was last heard of exporting contact lenses from Ghana.
On My Radio (1979).

SELLERS, Peter
Also see THE GOONS.

SHADOWS
Led by Hank Marvin on lead guitar, Bruce Welch on rhythm guitar and Brian Bennett on drums. Brian Bennett replaced Tony Meehan who joined Decca Records as an A & R man.

The original drummer, Terry Smart, left the band in 1958 to join the Merchant Navy and was replaced by Tony Meehan. In 1962 the original Jet Harris left to start a solo career and with Tony Meehan they had a hit with Applejack in 1963.

Brian 'Liquorice' Locking who joined in 1962 to play bass left the following year to become a Jehovahs Witness. In the early Seventies Marvin, Welch and friend John Farrar formed a trio and had a single UK top 30 hit and also produced If Not You for Olivia Newton- John. In 1973 Hank Marvin also became a Jehovahs Witness. John Rostill who replaced Locking in 1963, died in 1973 from accidental electrocution while playing guitar at his home studio. In 1975 the band represent the UK in the Eurovision Song Contest.

Hank Marvin now been living in Australia for ten years. Drummer Brian Bennett is now a film and television soundtrack composer and along with Marvin toured the country as Marvin, Bennett & Sons, including two of their sons in the band. Bruce Welch earned a reputation as an excellent guitarist and is now producer for Sir Cliff as well as planning an instrumental album of his own. Ex-Shadow Tony Meehan's problems with alcohol addiction has marred his career as a brilliant bass player and has had many jobs outside of music, recently running a market stall in Gloucester.

SHALAMAR

Howard Hewitt, the original vocalist, left in 1986 and was replaced by Sidney Justin, an ex-Los Angeles football player. Jody Watley had a solo success in 1987 with Looking For A New Love (No. 13 in 1987). She is now a major US dance and soul star in her own right winning the Best Newcomer Category at the Grammy Awards. Hewitt is now signed to Calibre Records in America and Expansion Records in England.

SHAM 69

The herberts from Hersham stomped all over the charts in the late Seventies before continued outbreaks of violence at the band's gigs curtailed their progress. They called it a day in 1980 but reformed in 1985. In the meantime Jimmy Pursey had busied himself producing new acts. Skinny Jimmy has also been snapped up by top designers to model their collections on the cat walk – a far cry from the days when school walls were daubed with Jimmy Is Our Leader
If The Kids Are United (1978).

SHANGRI-LAS

Formed in the early Sixties by two pairs of white sisters (the Ganser sisters were twins). Towards the end of their careers the trio began to play oldies tours in the US although Mary Ganser died of encephalitis. Marge

The Shadows

Sham 69

Autobiographies
Ten who have told it like it was

1 **Boy George**
   Take It Like A Man
2 **Ian Hunter**
   Diary Of A Rock n Roll Star
3 **Marianne Faithfull**
   Faithfull
4 **Connie Francis**
   Who's Sorry Now
5 **Gary Glitter**
   The Leader
6 **Jerry Lee Lewis**
   Killer
7 **Sandie Shaw**
   World At My Feet
8 **Ian Gillan**
   Child In Time
9 **Dave Davies**
   Kink
10 **Adam Faith**
   Act of Faith

Ganser died of an accidental overdose in 1976. In 1984 a Leader of the Pack musical was staged in New York. The Shangri-Las are still touring but with none of the original members.
Leader Of The Pack (1965).

SHANNON, Del
Although wealthy due to property investments Shannon still continued to tour throughout the Eighties. Alcohol and drugs took their toll in 1990 and Shannon took his own life with a rifle shot at his Santa Clarita Valley home in California.
Runaway (1961).

SHAPIRO, Helen
Had her first hit in 1961 when fourteen years old. Both You Don't know and Walkin' Back To Happiness spent three weeks at on top of the charts. Shapiro made a major career decision and veered much more towards stage musicals. In 1979 she starred in the musical The French Have a Song For It. A year later she starred as Nancy at the Albury Theatre in a revival of the hit musical Oliver. 1991 she teamed- up with Cliff Richard for a gospel music event. She also performs in cabaret touring regularly either with Sixties revival shows or singing jazz with Humphrey Littleton.
Walkin' Back To Happiness (1961).

Del Shannon

Showaddywaddy

SHAW, Sandie

Was only seventeen when she had her first No. 1 and had won the Eurovision Song Contest. Ten years later she was broke and waiting on tables in Soho. A revival with the help of her Buddhist faith and encouragment by Morrisey helped her discover new fans in the Nineties. In 1986 after several years of mainly domestic life she undertook a successful university tour. Five years later in 1991 she published her autobiography – The World at my Feet. She has released occasional singles to date and now works as a counsellor helping musicians who have difficulty handling the pressures of fame.

SHERMAN, Bobby

Julie Do You Love Me? was his hit in 1970. Thereafter he turned to television producing and directing. He also became an emergency medical technician and paramedic.

SHIRELLES

The group credited with being the founders of the girl-group sound continued to record until 1967. Shirley Alston made a belated comeback to showbusiness in 1970. In 1959 when Doris Jackson stood up and sang This Is Dedicated To The One I Love little did she know that 35 years later she would be accepting a Rhythm & Blues Foundation Heritage Award and singing the same song. The Shirelles still perform around the world with original singer Doris Jackson.
Will You Still Love Me Tomorrow (1961).

SHOWADDYWADDY

Showaddywaddy clocked up an amazing 23 top forty singles and 12 huge selling albums (including 3 platinum) following their initial appearance on television's New Faces talent programme. Buddy Gask and Duke Allured now perform in a similarly styled group called The Teddys. Most of the remaining members of the original line up are still rocking and rolling in their drapes and brothel creepers, reviving memories of Three Steps To Heaven, Hey Rock n Roll, Under The Moon Of Love and the rest of their footstomping hits.
Three Steps to Heaven (1975).

SIFFRE, Labi

Siffre had his roots in the black community of apartheid ridden South Africa. One of his biggest hits, It Must Be Love, was given a new lease of life by Madness in 1992. He started writing poetry and scripts in the late Eighties and has since made a strong and disturbing impact with performances on TV and Radio. His first book of poems – Nigger – was released in 1993 and his follow up in 1995 – Blood On The Page – followed the same powerful themes.

Labi Siffre

SIGUE SIGUE SPUTNIK

Created by former Generation X frontman Tony James, this manufactured band enjoyed a brief but well publicised existence scoring a top ten hit with their first single Love Missile F1-11 in 1986. James went on to join Sisters of Mercy, while Chris Cavenagh achieved more

success with Mick Jones and Big Audio Dynamite. Ten years on from the tabloid frenzy which surrounded their reported £4 million deal with EMI, there is now Sputnik – The Next Generation, youngsters who claim that their fresh legs can keep the energy levels high.

SIMON, Carly

Daughter of Richard Simon who founded the illustrious publishing house Simon & Schuster. Since her heyday in the mid Seventies she has written film scores for Heartburn and contributed songs to Karate Kid and her Let The River Run for the film Working Girl won her an Oscar.
You're So Vain (1972).

SIMONE, Nina

Don't Let Me Be Misunderstood and I Put A Spell On You were covered, in turn, by The Animals and Alan Price. Towards the end of the Sixties Simone became a leading member of the American Black Movement and recorded several songs which became anthems of the Civil Rights Movement. In 1968 she was back in the British and

Sigue
Sigue
Sputnik

American charts with a classic from the hit rock musical Hair – Ain't Got No, I Got Life.

SINATRA, Nancy & Lee Hazlewood

Hazlewood was originally billed as a country artist and is credited with the discovery of Duane Eddy. Unhappy with his life following the death of a girlfriend he moved to live in Sweden. His only notable work since has been to co-write and star in a film called Smoke. Nancy Sinatra wanted to become an actress but despite several roles never achieved mainstream success. She later wrote a biography of her father. The duo were briefly re-united in 1995 at the launch of Sinatra's book. Sinatra, now in her fifties, recently posed for Playboy magazine.

SINGING NUN

Born Jeannie Deckers in Belgium in 1928 Sister Luc-Gabrielle was better known as The Singing Nun. Her self-written song Dominique topped the American chart and sold over a million copies. The ensuing royalties were spent on foreign missions by her convent near Brussels in Belgium. Sister Luc-Gabrielle left the convent in Fichermont in 1966 and faded into obscurity until her suicide in Belgium in 1985.
Dominique (1963).

SINITTA

In 1997 she starred in What A Feeling with fellow Eighties popsters Luke Goss and Sonia and claims to have been celibate for some

Sinitta

time following years of heady showbiz party-hopping. Sinitta's life change continued with visits to church every Sunday and weekly bible classes since she attended London's Christian Life Centre in 1994. This didn't prevent her appearing naked in David Essex's musical Mutiny.
Toy Boy (1988).

SKIDS

See BIG COUNTRY.

SLADE

Four brummie lads got together to form one of the premier Glam Rock bands of the early Seventies. Noddy Holder, the singer with a rasping voice and mirrored top hat, led the boys into the charts with hit after hit: Coz I Luv You; Cum on Feel the Noize; and the obligatory Christmas missive Merry Xmas Everybody all reached No. 1. Noddy went into media work, initially with BRMB but now on Piccadilly Radio. He now lives in Manchester and makes TV appearances as well as making his acting debut in The Grimleys which resulted in him being offered more roles.

Drummer Don Powell suffered multiple injuries in a car crash in 1973 which also took the life of his fiancee. Powell became an antique dealer and Dave Hill, the guitarist who used to glide round the streets of his native Wolverhampton in a Rolls Royce with the number plate YOB 1, is still pounding out Slade's old hits with Powell under the name of Slade II – he has also become a Jehovahs Witness. Don Powell was working in a bar

Soap Stars

Ten who have got all sudsy

1 Nick Berry *Eastenders*
2 Anita Dobson *Eastenders*
3 Malandra Burrows *Emmerdale*
4. Sophie Lawrence *Eastenders*
5 Davy Jones *Coronation Street*
6 Peter Noone *Coronation Street*
7 Michelle Gayle *Eastenders*
8 Craig McLachlan *Neighbours*
9 Kylie and Jason *Neighbours*
10 Danni Minogue *Home & Away*

Slade

when Dave suggested they reform in 1992. He now lives in Brighton with his hotel owning partner

Guitarist Jimmy Lea qualified as a physiotherapist but is still involved with music – he produces heavy metal band Chrome Molly – and he still lives in Wolverhampton.

SLEDGE, Percy

Atlantic soul artist who founded his career on the 1966 million-seller When a Man Loves a Woman which elevated him to international stardom. His chart success was confined to the Sixties but he still remains a popular draw an the club circuit both in the States and in the UK.

SLY & The Family Stone

Sly Stone created Sly & The Family Stone in 1967. He married his girlfriend on stage in 1974 only to be divorced within four months. Two years earlier he had been convicted for possession of two 2lbs of cannabis and in 1976 he filed for bankruptcy. Drug problems persisted and in 1987 Sly served 3 monthsin

prison having been caught with a large quantity of cocaine. Unfortunately this sharp shock had little effect and the now drug dependent singer was arrested again shortly after his release. In 1992 he was offered the chance to resurrect his musical career but blew the record company's advance and never made it to the studio.
Dance To The Music (1968).

SMALL FACES

Steve Marriott on vocals and guitar, Ronnie Lane on bass, Ian McLagan on organ and Kenny Jones on drums formed mod icons the Small Faces. Marriot left the band in 1969 to team up with Peter Frampton to form The Herd and The Small Faces split. The remainder of the band get together to form The Faces with Rod Stewart.

In 1978 Kenny Jones joined The Who after Keith Moon's death and took on the fight to collect lost royalties from the Faces' heyday. He has also worked on an animated film which is based on the story part of the band's Ogden's Nut Gone Flake.

In 1991 Marriott died from smoke inhalation

Chris Norman of Smokie now and the whole band then (above)

after a fire at his 16th century cottage in Arkesden, Essex.

Ronnie 'Plonk' Lane formed Slim Chance which included Gallagher & Lyle. Numerous benefit gigs were held to raise funds for Lane but the disease MS caused his health to deteriorate and he lived in Texas with his third wife and children until his death on 4th June 1997 aged 51.

Itchycoo Park (1967).

SMOKIE

Enjoyed success with Mickie Most's RAK Label picking up silver, gold and platinum discs around the world before a four year split. They reunited for a successful benefit gig in aid of the victims of the Bradford City stadium disaster.

Chris Norman decided to go solo and was replaced by Alan Barton but in 1995 while on tour in Germany their tour bus careered off the road in a freak hail-storm. They still tour now with a new singer.

Living Next Door To Alice (Who the Fuck is Alice?) featuring the club circuit comedian

Roy Chubby Brown brought yet another new dimension to the band's history, repeating their top five success and selling over 200,000 copies. Peter Spencer and Chris Norman have since written chart hits for Kevin Keegan and the English World Cup squad. Norman is still solo (now on his 8th solo album) and was voted International Video Star Of The Year in 1994 by CMT Europe.

Living Next Door To Alice (1976).

SOFT CELL

Marc Almond on vocals and David Ball on keyboards made up this early Eighties duo. In 1990 Ball re-emerged as one half of the act Grid who had a few minor successes on the East-West label. Almond has since made a success of a solo career.
Tainted Love (1981).

Jimmy Sommerville

Film Stars

Ten who have been imortalised on celluloid

1. Jerry Lee Lewis *Great Balls Of Fire*
2. The Doors *The Doors*
3. The Beatles *Backbeat*
4. Jan & Dean *Dead Man's Curve*
5. Sid Vicious *Sid And Nancy*
6. The Dells *The Five Heartbeats*
7. Bubby Holly *The Buddy Holly Story*
8. Janis Joplin *The Rose*
9. Ike & Tina Turner *What's Love Got To Do With It*
10. Ritchie Valens *La Bamba*

1997 toured with What A Feeling and has starred in West End musicals including a year in Grease. Spent a season starring in the Lily Savage show and there are plans for a BBC sitcom TV series.
Youll Never Stop Me Loving You (1989).

Sonia now

SOMERVILLE, Jimmy
Shot to fame in 1984 when his falsetto squeal was first heard on Bronski Beat's top three hit Smalltown Boy. An equally successful spell as The Communards followed before Glaswegian Somerville scored hits as a solo performer in 1989/90. He has since taken time out from his high profile celebrity existence to 'live life as a gay man in the 90s'. He has also dabbled in film work acting, producing and most recently singing the part of a swallow in Channel 4's production of The Happy Prince shown on Christmas Day 1996. 1997 will see the release of a new album on Gut Records and live appearances in Paris and Lithuania.
You Make Me Feel (Mighty Real) (1990).

SONIA
Went from terraced house in Liverpool to national stardom courtesy of the Stock, Aitken and Waterman hit making factory. In

Sonny & Cher

David Soul

SONNY & CHER

The pair divorced in 1974 after over ten years together as a performing duo. Cher has continued to enjoy world wide popularity, both as a singer and Hollywood actress. Her credits include The Witches of Eastwick and Mask – the director of the latter described the experience of working with her as 'like being in a blender with an alligator'! Cher's stormy marriage to Greg Allman ended in divorce in 1979. Sonny returned to a successful career in record production. He was also elected mayor of Palm Springs, California before opening Palm Springs Restaurant with his fourth wife.

In 1991 he released his autobiography And The Beat Goes On and announced his intention to run for Alan Cranson's Senate seat in California. Three years later Sonny defeated Democrat Steve Cloot, 56% to 38%, to win California's 4th district congressional seat in the House of Representatives.

HE still has time for music and dabbles with recording and song-writing. He also has a studio built in his Palm Springs restaurant.

Cher has also shown a canny eye for business, selling millions of pounds worth of hairspray, beauty aids and fitness products.
I Got You Babe (1965).

SOUL, David

Moved to south west London after news headlines in America claiming that he had mis treated his wife. Since the Starsky & Hutch TV series of the Seventies, he has appeared in a number of TV films and directed an episode of Miami Vice. He released two films in 1994 – Pentathlon with Dolph Lundgren and Tides Of War – which he co-wrote and starred in.
Dont Give Up On Us (1976).

SOUTHLANDERS

Britain's longest lasting vocal group who in 1997 celebrated 44 years in the business. Original member Vernon Nesbeth still fronts the group who despite their long and successful career they are best remembered for I Am A Mole And I Live In A Hole.

SPANDAU BALLET

Martin Kemp suffered a brain tumour in February 1995 Gary Kemp, Martin Kemp, Tony Hadley, John Keeble and Steve Norman. Early Eighties new romantics built around Tony Hadley and the brothers Kemp who have all gone on to develop new careers post pop stardom. In 1997 Hadley released his first solo album since – he has included several covers including Duran

Duran's Save A Prayer which features Simon Le Bon on backing vocals. He has been performing live on a grand scale with a 75-piece orchestra on his Night Of The Proms arena tour, but also in more intimate club surroundings such as Ronnie Scotts. He collaborated on Tin Tin Outs top forty single Dance With Me and wrote the theme song for the football movie When Saturday Comes starring Sean Bean.

In 1988 the Kemp brothers played Ron and Reggie Kray in the movie The Krays. Martin Kemp is married to Shirlie (former Wham backing singer) and has been making films in America. He has also written a film script which he hopes will be taken up.

Gary Kemp also played Whitney Houston's manager in the 1992 hit film The Bodyguard has been writing a musical in conjunction with the writer of My Left Foot.

John Keeble plays drums for Tony Hadleys live shows and Steve Norman (sax) has been living in Spain for the past six years, having married a Spaniard.

True (1983).

Spandau Ballet

Sparks

SPARKS

Made up by the bizarre Mael brothers, Ron (the straight faced one with the stare) and Russell (the bouncy one with the mop of hair). They came out of Los Angeles but were better received in England. They moved to London in 1973 to release hit singles and albums Kimono My House and Propoganda. They adopted a change of style in the late Seventies to appeal to disco audiences. With the help of producer Georgio Moroder they succeeded with Number One Song In Heaven. Since then they have changed record label several times managing only one classic title – Gratuitous Sax and Senseless Violins. Now signed to Virgin Records they released a new album in 1997. Guitarist Adrian Fisher who played on the Kimono album has hit harder times and having lost everything now plays in seedy bars in Thailand, barely scratching a living.
This Town Ain't Big Enough For The Both Of Us (1974).

SPECTOR, Phil

Influential producer responsible for a unique sound associated with Sixties all girls groups, notably the Ronettes. In 1975 he survived two near-fatal car crashes and became very much a recluse, unwilling to talk about his work or appear publicly.

In 1981 he recorded a new album with Bette Midler and is in demand as a doyen of the music industry. He appeared in the London High Court in 1997 to finally win his 11 year battle to regain the rights to his song To Know Him Is To Love Him and was proved to be owed a substantial sum in back royalties which could grow like topsy as he is now to pursue the claim world-wide.

SPEDDING, Chris.

Shed his stage outfit as one of the Wombles to put on leathers for his Motor Biking which revved up to number 14 in 1975. Now works as a session musician and producer based in Los Angeles, where he moved in 1993.
Motor Biking (1975).

SPECIALS

Coventry group led by Terry Hall who gave mew life to Ska. Most of the orginal members are still involved in music. Keyboard player Gerry Dammers was was running a club in London's Rock Garden in 1993 and announced 'I'm going to go to Littlehome Studio and be independent of all record companies'. Terry Hall has a successful solo career and in 1997 released the album Ballard Of A Landlord on the Southsea Bubble Company label. The Specials were re-formed in 1995 led by original members Golding, Staples, Panter and Radiation, recording on Cuff Records.
Ghost Town (1981).

SPLIT ENZ

Neil Finn, Paul Hester and Nick Seymour went on to form Crowded House in 1985. Lead singer Tim Finn has since achieved a measure of success as a solo artist and has recently recorded an album with his brother Neil titled Finn. He also is part of Alt with Hothouse Flowers singer and songwriter Liam O'Maonlai. Neil Finn now lives with his family in his home country of New Zealand and is working in his home studio on his first solo album. Seymour lives in Ireland and has been touring with Deadstar. Paul Hester now lives in Melbourne where he has developed a pilot entertainment programme for TV and co-owns a restaurant called the Elmwood Beach House.
I Got You (1980).

Splodgenessabounds

SPLODGENESSABOUNDS

Beer swilling humour and non-sensical lyrics are still part of Max Splodge's recipe. They are still touring with Splodge himself returning in the guise of Ghengis Khan reincarnate.

Two Pints Of Lager And A Packet Of Crisps Please (1980).

Dusty Springfield

SPRINGFIELD, Dusty

Dubbed the White Negress by Cliff Richard, Springfield has recently celebrated 34 years as one of the world's finest vocalists. After nine top ten hits and world-wide success in the Sixties she had to endure a slump in fortunes during the Seventies before a partnership with the Pet Shop Boys returned her to the charts in 1987. Between 1974 and 1977 she did no recording work and admitted to taking too many tranquillisers and drinking too much. More success followed in 1989, again with the Pet Shop Boys, when In Private reached No. 14 in the charts.

In 1995 she underwent treatment for breast cancer in the Royal Marsden Hospital and returned to music with Wherever Would I Be? a duet with Daryl Hall which featured in the movie While You Were Sleeping.

You Don't Have To Say You Love Me (1966).

STAFFORD, Jim

Stafford was originally in a band called The Legends with two friends, including Kent Lavoie who went on to record in the Seventies as Lobo, and Gram Parsons. Stafford is perhaps best remembered for Spiders And Snakes which went on to sell over 2 million copies in the early Seventies. His pop music career ground to a halt in 1977 and he turned to acting, appearing in the Clint Eastwood film Any Which Way You Can in 1980. In the following years he went back to television and presented with Priscilla Presley on Those Amazing Animals. Today he lives near Branson, Missouri, a small town which has been transformed into a Las Vegas style night-club strip, with theatres owned and operated by The Osmonds, Tony Orlando and Jim Stafford. His Jim Stafford Theatre opened in 1991, and he performs there himself from May-December each year.

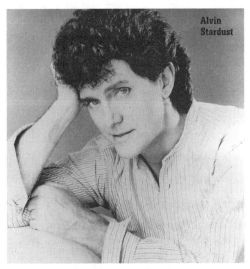

Alvin Stardust

STARDUST, Alvin

Started his career as plain Shane Fenton but at the height of his success quit performing and went into management/agency work, handling artists such as The Hollies and Lulu. 'Then I gave it all up and went off round the world ' he adds 'But when the money ran out, I came back home, re-formed The Fentones and set out playing authentic rock n roll in the British cabaret clubs.'

He transformed himself into the leather clad Alvin Stardust in the early Seventies and topped the charts with My Coo Ca Choo and Jealous Mind, among others.

Former husband of actress Liza Goddard, Stardust is a born again Christian who has since worked on TV as well as appearing in religious concerts.

Jealous Mind (1974).

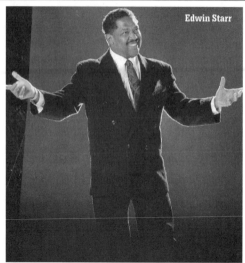

Edwin Starr

STARR, Edwin

Million-selling US chart topper with War (What Is It Good for)? He spends as much time writing and producing as performing and has penned several film scores. He is very active on the club and cabaret scene touring with his nine-piece band The Team.
War (1970).

STARR, Ringo

See The BEATLES.

STARSHIP

Although often overshadowed by Grace Slick, Mickey Thomas was the voice on their Eighties hits Jane, Sara and We Built This City and he now performs as Starship featuring Mickey Thomas.
We Built This City (1985).

Status Quo

STATUS QUO

The denim clad rockers have sold over 100 million records and have been around long enough to celebrate their thirtieth anniversary. Only Rick Parfitt and Francis Rossi remain from the original line up but Andrew Bown (keyboards) has been part of the phenomenon since 1976.

John Coghlan (drums) left in 1982 to concentrate on his own band called Diesel. Alan Lancaster (bass) only plays with the band on an ad hoc basis having relocated to Australia. He rejoined Quo to perform at the Live Aid concert.

Steeleeye Span

STEELEYE SPAN

For their 25th anniversary tour in 1997 the band were re-joined by Gay Woods who actually sang on their first recording. Their Album Time released the year before was the first album to hit the national chart for some time although Steeleye Span retain their popularity.

The first Steeleye Span line up included Ashley Hutchings (now a solo artist) and Terry Woods (now of The Pogues). Maddy Prior has been at the helm through many line up changes and has also worked with her husband and former bass player with Steeleye, Rick Kemp. She has also presented two radio series for Radio Two called In Good Voice.
All Around My Hat (1975).

STEELY DAN

Singles Do It Again and Rikki Don't Lose That Number are still held in high esteem despite making vey little chart impact in the mid Seventies. The band stopped touring in 1974 and finally broke up in 1980, but they could not resist the temptation to re-form some fifteen years later.

STEPPENWOLF

Steppenwolf's music featured extensively in the cult movie Easy Rider and brought their singles The Pusher and Born To Be Wild to world wide audiences. At one time there were three different versions of Steppenwolf touring the States all at the same time! The success was short lived and the group split up in 1972. In 1981 Rushton Morebe, the band's bass player, was killed in a car accident in Los Angeles. In 1993 long-time drummer Jerry Edmonton also died in a car accident in Santa Barbara, California. John Kay has managed to keep the group together in one form or another during the Nineties with various line-ups and now lives in Tennessee. He has published his own autobiography appropriately called Magic Carpet Ride.
Born To Be Wild (1969).

Cat Stevens

STEVENS, Cat

In a state of collapse and suffering from TB he spent three months in a sanatorium, where he had time to re-evaluate his work and life. Stevens became a Moslem convert and married a woman to whom he had never spoken and only seen at a London mosque. He changed his name to Yusef Islam in 1977 and retired from all aspects of making music to live the life of a recluse and shunning the world of showbusiness as much as possible.

In 1981 he financed the establishment of a Moslem school in north London and began to teach there. In 1993 he was appointed President of the Islamic Association of North London and is still living with his wife and five children at the Kilburn Islamic school he founded. After 18 years absence from music he released a new album in 1995 entitled The Life of the Last Prophet.
Morning Has Broken (1972).

STEWART, Al

Constant performing since the Sixties has allowed Stewart to build a valuable collection of vintage wines at his home in France. All a far cry from his beginnings as a member of the Sabres, backing band to a budding singer called Tony Blackburn.
Year Of The Cat (1977).

STEWART, Billy

Had one hit in the mid Sixties with Summertime. Stewart was killed in a traffic accident in North Carolina in January 1970.

RORY STORM & THE HURRICANES

Although never making the same impact as their peers, Rory Storm and his boys were one of the biggest acts during the Merseybeat boom. Rory went on to become a disc jockey but died in 1972. Tragically his mother discovered his body and died herself later the same night.

STRAWBS

Initially an acoustic folk band who over the years drifted more towards rock. Rick Wakeman (Yes) and Sandy Denny (Fairport Convention) were also members at one time. When Wakeman left to join Yes they recruited Blue Weaver who was formerly with Amen Corner. Singer Sandy Denny fell down a flight of stairs in April 1978, suffered a brain haemorrhage and lapsed into a coma – she died four days later..

The band had split after Part of The Union had been a huge success in 1973. Other members Hudson and Ford hit the top 20 with Pick Up The Pieces later in same year then as the Monks in 1979 charted again with Nice Legs, Shame About The Face. Ford emigrated to America, while Hudson rejoined The Strawbs and is still with them today. Blue Weaver became a session musician.

A re-formed Strawbs continued on briefly but failed to make any impact without the direction of their founder Dave Cousins who took over as Controller of Radio Tees. Cousins played the folk clubs and moved to local radio in Devon until the mid Eighties when he reformed The Strawbs.

The Nineties have seen a flurry of Strawbs releases with a combination of new material and re-releases.

The current line-up is fluid but includes Tony Hooper (who left 1972, disillusioned with their increasing rockiness), Mick Weaver, Richard Hudson, Rod Demick and even Mary Hopkin *Part Of The Union (1973)*.

STRAY CATS

Drummer Jim McDonnell spent nine years married to Britt Ekland although he was seventeen years her junior.

Their most successful years were 1980-81 with Stray Cats and Stray Cats Strut.

In 1988 lead vocalist Brian Setzer played Eddie Cochran in the Ritchie Valens' biopic La Bamba. He then released his own solo album and in 1996 formed his own orchestra to perform string versions of rockabilly pop standards and signed to Hollywood Records. Slim Jim started a new band called Cheap Dates which also consists of Jeff Skunk Baxter of the Doobie Brothers.

STYLE COUNCIL

See THE JAM.

Stylistics

STYLISTICS

Formed in 1968 in Philadelphia this soft soul band featured Eddie Kendricks who went on to solo success in later years. In 1975 the Best Of Stylistics album shot to number one with sales of over one million copies. The Band still tours the world although they are now only a trio – original members James Smith and James Dunn Junior left the band in the Seventies.

Can't Give You Anything (But My Love) (1975).

Drug death

Ten who have died on drugs

1 Gram Parsons (Byrds)
2 Tommy Bolin (Deep Purple)
3 Jim Morrison (Doors)
4 Andy Gibb
5 Sid Vicious
6 Jimi Hendrix
7 Janis Joplin
8 Frankie Lyman
9 Billy Mercia (New York Dolls)
10 Paul Gardiner (Tubeway Army)

STYX

Having achieved a hit with Babe in 1980 they broke up in the mid Eighties before re-forming in 1991. Drummer and co-founder John Panazzo – he formed the band with his brother Chuck – died on July 16th 1996 from cirrhosis of the liver.

SUMMER, Donna

Queen of the disco who has now been at the top for twenty years. She caused a storm in 1976 with her erotic Love To Love You Baby followed by a succession of dance hits and nine top tens. Summers topped the UK dance charts recently with a re-mixed version of her 1977 hit I Feel Love. Now also an accomplished artist, her work has been exhibited in galleries throughout America. Nine of her paintings and sketches have recently been on show in the lobby of the Tennessee Performing Arts Centre.

Love To Love You Baby (1976).

SUPERTRAMP

In 1982 Roger Hodgson (guitarist) left to start a solo career but briefly re-joined the band in 1986. He now lives in Nevada City, California and released his third solo album in 1997 which features versions of Supertramp's three biggest hits. The current line up touring the world are Rick Davies, John Helliwell, Bob Siebenberg and Mick Hart who was formerly with Crowded House.

Dreamer (1975).

SUPREMES

Legendary Motown female pop group who originally featured Diana Ross, Mary Wilson and Florence Ballard.

In 1967 Ballard was dismissed and replaced by Cindy Birdsong. Despite a $160,000 lump sum settlement from Motown, she filed an unsuccessful $8.5 million lawsuit against them in 1970 claiming that she was maliciously ousted. She hit financial hard times and was separated from her husband, which left her on welfare. In a sad tale of neglect, she pawned her jewellery, sold her furniture and became a recluse. Ballard died after a heart attack on February 22nd 1976 at the age of 32. She had taken pills for her blood pressure and had been drinking.

Diana Ross made her final live appearance with the Supremes and introduced her replacement – Jean Terrell – who stepped into the breach the following day. Cindy Birdsong quit in 1972 to devote more time to her home and marriage.

Wilson officially ceased to be a Supreme in 1977 but continued as a solo performer and recording artist, author, actress and mother! In 1983 Wilson released a book called Dream Girl: My Life as a Supreme. In 1994 Wilson

was seriously injured in a car accident on which has also resulted in the death of her 14 year old son.

Jean Terrell re-joined later members Sherrie Payne and Lynda Laurence to perform as The Supremes in Los Angeles in the mid Seventies – ironically Cindy Birdsong was in the audience.

Diana Ross meanwhile has established herself as an international star and recently celebrated her thirtieth anniversary in showbusiness, published her memoirs, produced and starred in a film for ABC and is touring again for the first time in three years. *Baby Love (1964).*

SUTCH, Screaming Lord

Now in his mid-fifties, Sutch still provides one of the most entertaining live shows. However, he now has to fit live appearances in between his hectic schedule dreaming up policies for his Monster Raving Loony Party.

SWEET

Seventies Glam Rockers whose outrageous stage show meant that they were banned from playing at many venues due to the so-called sexual nature of their act. Lead singer

Sweet

Brian Connolly left but the group continued to tour more as a heavy-metal band. He later formed Brian Connolly's Sweet but with none of the original members in the band. Brian Connolly died February 9th 1997 of kidney failure – a television documentary the year before had highlighted his fight for health.

Andy Scott now lives in Wiltshire and having moved to slow down a bit is once again touring extensively with his band Andy Scott's Sweet. Between times he can be found in his local, The Woodbridge Inn, or out on his best mate's 50ft boat with his wife Maddy.

Mick Tucker (drums) is presently retired from the music business and is unfortunately suffering from Leukaemia.

Steve Priest has now lived in Los Angeles for fifteen years and has written a book on his days in the band as well as writing songs for a future album release. His wife is heavily involved in the music business and has worked with Tina Turner and Michael Jackson.

A very early member, Frank Torpey, lives very close to Mick Tucker but they only recently spoke for the first time in 29 years. Although he released a CD a couple of years ago, Topley can be found playing his local pubs in Hertfordshire.
Blockbuster (1973).

SWING OUT SISTER

Although they have achieved limited success in the UK in recent years, they sold in excess of 600,000 albums in Japan in 1996 and won the best single award in the same country for their No. 1 hit Now You're Not Here.
Breakout (1986).

SWINGING BLUE JEANS

Ray Ennis, Ralph Ellis, Les Braid, Norman Kuhlke made up the Swinging Blue Jeans and are best known for Hippy Hippy Shake and You're No Good. Ray Ennis (lead singer) left the group in 1966 and was replaced by Terry Silvester who joined The Hollies when the group split up in 1968.

In 1973 Ennis and Braid re-formed the group with a new line-up. They are the only original member still appearing with the band which is still going strong on the nostalgia circuit.

Norman Kuhlke went into the building trade in Bath and Ralph Ellis found employment with an insurance company.
Hippy Hippy Shake (1963).

SYLVESTER

Disco star with high pitched voice famous for You Make Me Feel (Mighty Real) in 1978. Died ten years later from AIDS.

SYREETA

Famous as the secretary who became Stevie Wonder's wife and an internationally known artist with Your Kiss Is Sweet in 1975. In the early Eighties she withdrew from the music scene to raise her family but emerged later in a. duet with Billy Preston (With You I'm Born Again).

T-Rex and Marc Bolan memorial

T-REX

Originally formed by Marc Bolan and Steve Took. In 1969 Took left and was replaced by Mickey Finn. Steve Curry joined in 1970 on bass and in the following year Bill Legend joined on drums. Marc Bolan split from his wife in 1974, had mild heart attack and the band broke up. He faded from the music scene and made a move into TV. Immortality was sealed in 1977 when Bolan's car left the road on a bend at Barnes Common, London, and crashed into a tree. Bolan was killed two weeks before his 30th birthday and the site of his death is a shrine for Bolan fans.

In 1980 Bolans first partner, Steve Took, having spent a royalty cheque on the purchase of morphine and magic mushrooms choked to death on a cherry after the mushrooms numbed any sensation in his throat. Steve Curry was killed in 1981 when his car veered off the road as he returned to his home in Valderama.

Mickey Finn is now 50 and unemployed. Bill Legend is also in his fifties, lives in Essex and like Finn is unemployed. Gloria Jones, the driver of Bolan's car when he wsas killed, lives in Philadelphia while son Rolan has become a rap singer in Los Angeles with his own band called The Brothers Of Bounce.
Hot Love (1971).

TALKING HEADS

David Byrne, Tina Weymouth and Chris Franz met while at Rhode Island School of Design in 1970. They formed Talking Heads in 1975. Later without Byrne they also became Tom-Tom Club for hits including Wordy Rappinghood (No. 7 in 1981). Talking Heads officially split in 1991.

Since 1988 Byrne has been involved with the Luaka Bop record label which has an emphasis on music from around the world. Recent releases have been Cuban and Brazilian classics. He has made a documentary film about a Brazilian village and has become recognised as an accomplished photographer with his work published in major magazines and exhibited around the world. He lives on Rhode island, is married to Adella Bonny Lutz and they have a daughter called Malu Valentine. The other two have reunited under the name The Heads.
Road To Nowhere (1985).

James Taylor then and now (below)

TAYLOR, James

Now 49, he released his first album for five years in 1997. His past includes a period of serious

drug addiction and a marriage to Carly Simon which floundered because of his habit. He now spends half the year touring and the remaining six months holed up on Marthas Vineyard.
You've Got A Friend (1971).

TEARS FOR FEARS

Formed by friends Curt Smith and Roland Orzabal with Ian Stanley, hailing from Bath. Mad World (No. 3 in 1982) was their first hit but are better known for Everybody Wants To Rule the World (No.2 in 1985). Their 1989 song Woman In Chains proved to be the launching pad for singer Oleta Adams who added backing vocals to the hit – she later scored a hit with Get There in 1991, the year the band announced they were going their separate ways. Orzabal continued under the name of Tears For Fears while Smith signed a solo deal with Mercury and is now living in New York.

In 1995 Smith split from Mercury to join Epic records and has formed a new band called Mayfield who have now released their first album but are without a major distribution deal.

Orzabal started his own production company called Bread and Buddha. Ian Stanley took a job in the A & R department at East West Records.

TEMPTATIONS

Motown giants who have had a succession of singers who have gone on to their own sol success. In 1971 Eddie Kendricks leaves for a solo career (Keep On Truckin No. 8 in 1973). Kendricks died of lung cancer at the Baptist Medical Centre in 1992, a year after having a lung removed. David Ruffin had joined the group in 1963 but left in 1968 to pursue a solo career (Walk Away From Love No. 10 in 1976). In 1987 he was convicted of cocaine possession and in 1991 he died of a drug overdose in the hospital of the University of Pennsylvania.

Paul Williams, who had left the group in 1971 but continued to supervise the groups choreography, was found dead in his car in 1973. His celebrity boutique had failed so he shot himself in the head.

What was left of the Temptations backed Hollywood star Bruce Willis with his version of Under the Boardwalk.

Melvin Franklin died in April 1995 of heart failure following years of suffering diabetes.

Otis Williams is now the only original member and continues to lead today's version of the group.

10cc

Graham Gouldman, Eric Stewart, Lol Creme, and Kevin Godley were 10cc. Gouldman had previously been a successful songwriter in the Sixties with hit songs such as the Yardbirds' For Your Love and No Milk Today for Hermans Hermits to his credit. 10cc enjoyed years of chart success in the Seventies from Donna in 1972 to Dreadlock Holiday in 1978. By the late Seventies Godley and Creme were operating as a duo and they finally found mainstream appeal with Under Your Thumb and then Wedding Bells in 1981. They also developed an increasingly successful career as innovative music video directors and producers. They invented the 'gizmo' which when attached to the bridge of a guitar could create sounds of other instruments. They were also the first producers to use morphing on video which shows images melting into each other. In 1990 Godley was co-founder of the UK environmental organisation Ark.

In 1983 Gouldman re-emerged as one half of Common Knowledge which then became Wax – both units formed in partnership with Andrew Gold. In the early Nineties Gouldman and Stewart re-united as 10cc and in 1995 played an acoustic set at the Lloyds building in the City of London.
I'm Not In Love (1975).

TEN POLE TUDOR

Reached number 6 in 1979 with Who Killed Bambi then bounced (literally) back into the charts two years later with Swords Of A Thousand Men. Now equally as active and enthusiastic as presenter of Channel 4s futuristic game show Crystal Maze.

TEN YEARS AFTER

One of the most successful British rock bands ever to tour America, their rendition of Goin' Home at the Woodstock Festival proved to be one of the highlights of the film of the event. In 1973 Alvin Lee took time off from the group to build his own studio at his Berkshire home and to concentrate on a solo recording career, releasing the first of several solo albums. Ric Lee formed his own production company,

while Leo Lyons also went into production and later worked with British rock group UFO.

Meanwhile, Chick Churchill (keyboards) joined Chrysalis Records as an executive and now runs a picture framing business and art gallery in Goring, Berkshire. Ten Years After were resurrected again for a tour in 1997.
Love Like A Man (1970).

TEX, Joe

Seventies disco king who changed his name to Yusef Hazziez and became a spiritual lecturer in the Muslim faith. He also owned a ranch in Texas and was a big supporter of the Houston Oilers. He died August 1982 of heart attack.
Ain't Gonna Bump No More (With No Big Fat Woman) (1977).

Thin Lizzy

THIN LIZZY

Irish rockers whose all time classic Whiskey In The Jar helped to establish them both as recording stars and one of the best live acts of their day. They split in 1983.

Guitarist Gary Moore and Phil Lynott continued to make music together but in 1986 Lynott died of heart failure and pneumonia following septicaemia at Salisbury General Infirmary in Wiltshire. His wife Caroline and father- in-law, Leslie Crowther, were by his bedside. The remaining members of Thin Lizzy re-formed for a one-off gig as a tribute. Gary Moore has continued to chart as a solo artist, his greatest success being the haunting Parisienne Walkways (No. 8 in 1979).
My Boy: The Phillip Lynott Story written by his mother on the 10th anniversary of his death was published in 1996.

THOMPSON TWINS

Formed in 1977 by Tom Bailey and some of his Chesterfield Grammar School friends. However it was as a trio with later additions Alannah Currie and former roadie Joe Leeway that the Thompson Twins became best known. Joe Leeway gave up the pop star life in 1986 and retired to Los Angeles to settle down and begin a new life writing music for video games and film.

In the late Eighties Currie and Bailey had a son and did some writing and production for former Blondie singer Debbie Harry.

The last album released under the Thompson Twins name came out in 1991, although a greatest hits album was released in 1996. The 1991 release of the single Come Inside as Feedback Max reached No. 1 in the dance charts.

In 1993 the duo teamed up with engineer Keith Fernley to forge a new musical direction under the name of Babble and one of their songs featured in the Dan Ackroyd film The Cone-Heads. They disbanded shortly afterwards, since when Bailey has involved himself with writing film soundtracks.
Hold Me Now (1983).

THREE DEGREES

Prince Charles' favourite group headed by Sheila Ferguson who left to pursue a solo career is now a writer (of cookery books) and actress. The other original two members still perofrm in cabaret.
When Will I See You Again (1974).

THUNDERCLAP NEWMAN

Enjoyed massive success with Something In The Air which topped the British charts in the summer of 1969. They recorded one album – Hollywood Dream. Andy Newman and John Keen both recorded well-received solo albums, while Jimmy McCulloch found recording and performing success with Blue, Stone the Crows and Paul McCartney's band Wings. In 1979 he was found dead in tragic, yet unexplained circumstances in a London flat.

TILLOTSON, Johnny

Responsible for the 1960 hit Poetry In Motion however failure to repeat the success coupled with his National Service Army call up effectively ended his pop career. He then returned to his country roots but was unable to re-establish himself and took to cabaret where he can still be found today. He currently plays approximately 230 days a year from Lake Tahoe to Las Vegas.

TIGHT FIT

A group of session musicians put together to sing a trio of top ten successes in the early Eighties although the Tight Fit seen in public did not actually record the songs and never performed live. Several of the musicians and singers have now formed a live act called New Tight Fit and are working theatres, nightclubs and arenas.
The Lion Sleeps Tonight (1982).

TIMELORDS

See KLF.

TINY, TIM

Born Herbert Khaury he became better known as the falsetto voice which was Tiny Tim. He married dancer Miss Vicki live on Johnny Carson's American TV show in 1969 but the marriage ended in divorce. He faded from the limelight to become a novelty act playing obscure New York bars. Fighting a severe weight problem, he continued to play in small venues until his death in 1997 from a heart attack.

TORNADOS, The

The Tornadoes were put together by independent UK producer Joe Meek. In 1967 Meek fatally shoots his landlady, Mrs Violet Shinten, at his 304 Holloway Road flat before turning the gun on himself.

The Tornadoa had become the first British group ever to get a number one in the USA and their hit Telstar has now sold in excess of nine million copies. The original drummer and founder member Clem Cattini still fronts a group bearing the same name as well as being a top session musician. He has also played on over forty No. 1 records, backing such artists as Michael Jackson, The Bay City Rollers and Cliff Richard. The original organ player, Roger La Verne, became an actor and singer in his own right. Following an operation on the tendons in his hands, he still performs as a successful concert pianist and after dinner speaker. Guitarist George Bellamy moved to Devon to become a builder, but probably the best known Tornado, Heinz, went on to record the massive hit Just Like Eddy as a solo performer. Stuart Taylor has become business manager to Peter Green (ex- Fleetwood Mac).

In 1991 the original Tornados re-united for the first time in 30 years.
Telstar (1962).

TOURISTS
See EURYTHMICS.

TOYAH
The throaty voice belonging to the one time queen of punk who yelled I Want To Be Free now provides the narration on children's TV series Brum. She has also appeared on mainstream programmes such as Antiques Roadshow and the Holiday Programme as well as taking acting roles in film and TV plays. Married to Bob Fripp (King Crimson), they live in a small manor house just outside Salisbury which was previously owned by the artist Cecil Beaton.
I Want To Be Free (1981).

TRAVOLTA, John
The film Grease provided four top ten outings for actor Travolta (three with Olivia Newton John). After a quiet spell he has re-emerged as one of Hollywoods elite – commanding $20 million dollars a film – and a cool property in films such as Tarantino's Pulp Fiction.
Youre The One That I Want (1978).

TREMELOES
In 1966 lead singer Brian Poole split from The Tremeloes and Alan Howard, the bass player, left the music business in 1966 to establish a dry-cleaning business in Barking – he was replaced in the band by Len Chip-Hawkes.

In 1972 Ricky West was injured in a car crash and left the group. In 1975 Alan Blakley decided to leave, which at that time left just two original members.

The new Tremeloes – Rick Westwood, Hawkes, Munden and new member Vic Elms (formerly with Christie of Yellow River fame, which ironically The Tremeloes had produced) – re-formed to tour and spend most of their time combining engagements in Holland, Germany and Scandinavia as well as being active on the British cabaret circuit.

In 1983 Hawkes left to start a solo vocal

career and front his own band. Dave Munden, and Rick Westwood still perform in cabaret. Alan Blakley died from cancer in June 1996. See also BRIAN POOLE

Troggs

TROGGS
Formed in Andover, Hampshire in 1966 by Reg Presley (Ball), Chris Britton, Pete Staples and Ronnie Bond (Bullis).

In their first year the band enjoyed four top ten singles in Britain with Wild Thing being their first chart entry. In 1969 Staples was replaced by Tony Murray and in 1972 Richard Moore replaced Britton who moved to Portugal to start his own night-club. Bond died at the age of 51 at Winchester General Hospital on November 13th 1992.

Presley and Britton remain the only original members of the band still performing today (they played at Sting's wedding).

In 1994 Wet Wet Wets version of the Trogg's 1967 hit Love Is All Around featured in the hugely successful film Four Weddings And A Funeral. Reg Presley reportedly spent some of his resulting royalties researching the corn circle phenomenon. Now 55, Presley has been married for 35 years and is also a grandfather, and claimed that they started a world tour in 1966 and havent finished it yet. But despite the newly found wealth from the contemporary success of his song Love Is All Around he still lives in a semi in Andover and mixes socially with friends made well before stardom.

TURNER, Ike & Tina
Ike Turner and Annie Mae Tina Bullock formed a formidable sould duo in the Sixties and their classic – Nutbush City Limits, written by Tina in 1973 – sold a million copies They had earlier been successful with River Deep Mountain High. In 1976 they announce

that not only was their musical partnership over but so too was their stormy marriage. Ike ended up in prison and suffered from drugs problems but since then has continued to record and has emerged as a leading producer. Tina became one of the most dynamic performers of her time and was an international superstar as a solo performer when most of her contemporaries had retired from live performances. A film was released in 1996 about their life aptly called What's Love Got To Do With It?

TURTLES

One of the most entertaining and humorous groups to come out of the flower power era. When the group broke up in 1970 band members Mark Volman and Howard Kaylan joined Frank Zappa and the Mothers of Invention. In 1972 as a double act they toured Europe and America and worked on sessions with Marc Bolan but broke up to devote their energies to broadcasting on their own radio show. When they re-formed the band became better known as Flo And Eddie and they were successful producers. (They had called themselves The Phlorescent Leech And Eddie due to contractual problems that prevented them from using their own names!). In addition to

their wacky radio humour the duo have also provided voices for Dirty Duck and music for Strawberry Shortcake and The Care Bears. They have now been touring as The Turtles (featuring Flo and Eddie) since 1984 when they finally regained the rights to the name.

TWINKLE

Lynne Annette Ripley from Surbiton in Surrey became the bikers favourite when Terry made No. 4 in 1965. She retired to life as a housewife but re-emerged seven years later with her version of I'm A Believer. Married to actor Graham Rogers (TVs Milk Tray man!) their son Michael is now The Weatherman hitting it big making rave music. Twinkle herself is now back in the swing, appearing at Sixties shows.
Terry (1965).

TWITTY, Conway

Conway Twitty became a multi millionaire despite not making a penny from his first single It's Only Make Believe which sold over eight million copies and was No. 1 in 22 countries – in his early days he signed away his rights to a share of the royalties. The story since then was astounding with 52 No. 1 hits as a country artist which earned him a fortune which has been invested into his own travel agency, a publishing company, four baseball teams and even Twitty City, a Nashville based entertainment complex which spreads over nine acres.
It's Only Make Believe (1958).

TYLER, Bonny

Tyler's distinctive voice came as a result of a throat operation in 1976 and became her trademark when Lost In France entered the charts in the same year. Seven years later her Total Eclipse of the heart topped the American chart and sold over 5 million copies world-wide. She was voted Female Artist Of The Year in Germany and her song Limelight was used as the German national theme tune for the 1996 Olympics.

She now lives in the Mumbles, Swansea, a is signed to East West Records and back touring.
Total Eclipse Of The Heart (1983).

Ike and Tina Turner

ULTRAVOX

Throughout the Eighties they enjoyed a stream of chart successes, the most famous of all being Vienna in 1981 with its atmospheric video. Midge Ure, former member of Slik (Forever and Ever a 1976 No. one), is now solo and has a home recording studio by the Thames in London and in the basement in his house on the tiny Caribbean island of Monserrat, where he had to clear away the damage wreaked by a passing hurricane. His most recent album, Pure, was released in 1996. Ure Collaborated with Bob Geldof on Band Aid and received a grammy for his work with the Princes Trust. He has also become an adept producer of videos and has worked with Phil Lynott and Bananarama. Former member of Gary Numan's Tubeway Army, and to many the backbone to Ultravox, Billy Currie (keyboards) is writing film music.

Vienna was kept from the number one spot by Joe Dolce's Shaddap You Face in 1981.

UNDERTONES

Led by Feargal Sharkey on vocals the Undertones stormed out of Londonderry at the start of the Eighties. The group disbanded in 1983 and Sharkey joined ex-Depeche Mode and Yazoo keyboard player Vince Clark to become The Assembly. In 1993 Sharkey charted with I've Got News for You and then subsequently joined Capone Records as A&R Executive, before going on to head up the new interactive record label the Multimedia Company ESP in December 1994.

My Perfect Cousin (1980).

UPSIDE DOWN

Four average guys plucked from obscurity by two ambitious businessmen determined to create The Next Big Thing. The rapid rise to fame and back again started with the narrowing down of 7,000 applicants to four, who were then packaged, scraped three top twenty entries, rebelled and then were systematically binned. The quartet had become concerned about their mates' reaction to their growing popularity within the gay community.

Despite this manufactured assault on the music market, Upside Down are still making music together and hoping for a less contrived assault on the charts.

Uriah Heep

URIAH HEEP

Heavy metal band from London named after the Charles Dickens character. Lead singer David Byron, having been fired from the band in 1976 due to his excessive drinking, died of a heart attack in 1985. He had recorded four solo albums and one with Rough Diamond.

In the late 1970s Mick Box decided to disband Heep, however it wasn't long before they were on the road again and in 1995 they celebrated their 25th anniversary.

Box has been there throughout, Lee Kerslake has been drumming since 1972 while Trevor Bolder has been on bass since 1976 with just one year away when he played with Wishbone Ash.

John Lawton now sings in a rock covers band called Gun Mill.

Ricky Valance

Vanilla Ice

VALANCE, Ricky

Tell Laura I Love Her topped the charts in 1960 but is memorable enough to earn Valance a living on the revival circuit nearly forty years later.

VALENS, Ritchie

Best known for the million-selling Donna (coupled with La Bamba) – a song he had written for his high school sweetheart Donna Ludwig. Valens died on February 3rd 1959 in the same plane crash that took the lives of Buddy Holly and Big Bopper. They had just taken off from Mason City airport when bad weather forced the plane to crash into nearby fields at Ames, Iowa.

VALENTINE, Dickie

Died in 1971 in a car accident. He had established himself as a Fifties heart throb before rock & roll took a grip on the charts. At the time of his death he had finally managed to resurrect his career as an all round entertainer.
Finger Of Suspicion and Christmas Alphabet – (1954 & 1955).

VANILLA ICE

Now owns and runs a bicycle hire shop on Miami Beach having blown the millions that he earned from world-wide success as a rapper.
Ice Ice Baby (1990).

Village People

VAUGHAN, Frankie

Eleven hits in a decade from 1954 established Frankie Vaughan as an all round entertainer who continues to perform on the cabaret circuit. Lives in London with his wife Stella.

VEE, Bobby

A tragic twist of fate was the launching pad for Vee's career. When the plane carrying Buddy Holly, Richie Valens and the Big Bopper crashed on the way to their next engagement in Minnesota, the promoters decided to continue with the show and asked for local talent to perform. 15 year old Bobby Vee took the stage and

Bobby Vee

became a star. Take Good Care Of My Baby (his first American chart-topper, which sold a million copies), Run To Him and The Night Has A Thousand Eyes were among his hits. From 1970 he recorded less frequently and dropped out of sight, later to attempt a comeback under his real name of Robert T Velline. Vee performes on the nostalgia circuit with regular visits to Britain where he stars in Sixties revival shows. He established his own recording studio based just outside St Cloud, Minnesota.
Rubber Ball (1961).

VELVET UNDERGROUND

Sterling Morrison, although not as well known as Lou Reed and John Cale, left in 1971 and became a teacher, earning a doctorate in Medieval Studies at the

University of Texas. He also qualified for his Captain's license on the Houston Ship Canal before his death in August 1995. Lou Reed and John Cale stuck to music!

VILLAGE PEOPLE

Jacques Morali, who formed the group having sold over 10 million records with this previous band, The Ritchie Family, died from AIDS in 1991 aged 41. Based on the All-American Macho Man myth of Cowboy, Indian, Leatherman, Soldier and Policeman, The Village People have since sold over 28 million albums and earned platinum discs in 35 countries. Victor Willis, the Policeman, was involved a bizarre incident in Nevada when a woman claimed that he had falsely imprisoned her. Glen Hughes (the leather-clad biker) ironically gained employment as a despatch rider. They reformed in 1987 and have toured ever since. *YMCA (1978).*

VINCENT, Gene

During a British concert tour with Eddie Cochran, Vincent was badly injured when Cochran's car crashed at Chippenham in Wiltshire. Cochran was killed outright and Vincent never really recovered from the accident. Dogged by financial problems brought on by bad management, he took to the bottle and by 1969 he was a wreck, severely overweight and deep in debt. Gene Vincent died on 12th October 1971 from heart failure. *Be Bop A Lula (1956).*

Gene Vincent

VINTON, Bobby

Vinton is now living in semi-retirement but is still able to command large fees for live appearances. He has also opened the Bobby Vinton Blue Velvet Theatre in Branson. The film American Werewolf in London featured his song Blue Moon and in 1989 Blue Velvet was used in the film of the same name and also in a television advert which brought him unexpectedly back into the top ten.

WALKER, Junior & The ALL STARS

Piano and sax playing Motown singer Junior Walker died of cancer at Butler Creek, Missouri on November 23rd 1995, aged 53. Although he only achieved limited success on his own, he guested with Foreigner on their Eighties hit Urgent and scored a succession of classic hits in America's R & B charts.
Road Runner(1966).

WALKER, Scott

See THE WALKER BROTHERS.

Scott Walker

WALKER BROTHERS

British-based Americans Scott Engel, John Naus and Dave Leeds produced several of the Sixties biggest hits – Make It Easy On Yourself and The Sun Ain't Gonna Shine Anymore, were both chart topping million sellers. From 1969 onwards Scott Walker went into semi-reclusion making only the occasional live appearance.

In 1975 against all expectations the trio got together again and in the following year No Regrets reached No. 7 in the UK charts. The re-formed Walker Brothers then split again and Dave Leeds severed all connections with the music business. He wrote a mad detective novel and worked in photography before starting a well publicised business in London – Sand Magic – making models from sand! When he gave this up, he returned to working as a motorcycle courier and is currently living with his family in Essex.

Naus has finally quit the UK to live back in the States after an abortive tour with Screaming Lord Such.

Engel spent three years studying fine art at Byamshaw College in London before releasing a new solo album, Tilt in 1995. In the early Nineties he had also been involved in writing and singing for films – the latest being To Have And To Hold with a Nick Cave produced soundtrack album.
The Sun Ain't Gonna Shine Anymore (1966).

Clifford T Ward

WARD, Clifford T

Although Multiple Sclerosis has now robbed this former schoolteacher of his co-ordination and makes it difficult for him to speak, it has not dampened his enthusiasm for music. With the help of independent label Graduate Records he managed to record an album in 1994 with an introduction supplied by Cliff Richard.

Ward now has to survive on meagre state benefits and the occasional royalty cheque from his melodic Seventies ballads.
Gaye (1973).

Geno Washington

WASHINGTON, Geno & The RAM JAM BAND

Brought to the UK from his native Indiana by the US Air Force, he was first inspired to sing by a Shane Fenton (aka Alvin Stardust) concert. At the peak of his success Geno returned to America, disgusted by the manipulation in the business.

He returned ten years later reuniting with former members of his Ram Jam Band and he has since established himself as a much in demand act. His powerful live performances keep the band on the road.

WATERS, Muddy

An R&B legend and blues musicians who in 1980 collected his sixth Grammy award for best ethnic or traditional recording. In 1983 Muddy Waters died of a heart attack in his sleep at home in Chicago.

WATSON, Johnny Guitar

Died on 17th May 1995.

WEEDON, Bert

Guitar hero to many, and author of the bestselling *Play In A Day*, the book that launched many a guitarists career. Weedon is now in his seventies and still strumming away some sixty years on from his first gig. *Guitar Boogie Shuffle (1959)*.

WHAM!

Duo George Michael and Andrew Ridgeley officially split in 1986 after a run of ten top ten hits including three number ones. Since then Michael has pursued an incredibly successful solo career while Ridgeley moved to Monaco to concentrate on a future of semi-retirement, motor racing and acting.

Ridgeley married Karen Woodward of

Bananarama and released a solo album in 1990 from which the single Shake barely scraped into the UK top 100 but reached number 13 in Australia. Ridgeley now lives in Cornwall with his wife.

WELLS, Mary

One of Tamla Motown's most successful artists. My Guy, her best known hit, was re-released in 1972 when once again it reached the British top twenty. Wells married songwriter Cecil Womack and has virtually retired from the music business to concentrate on family life.
My Guy (1964).

WEST, Keith

Born Keith Hopkins and from Dagenham in Essex. Earned an Ivor Novello award for his Grocer Jack (called Excerpt from a Teenage Opera) in 1967. Now lives in Weybridge and works as a Marketing Director for Burns Guitars but still find time to write jingles. The full version of the Opera has now finally been released – thirty years later!

WHITE PLAINS

This band evolved from the Flowerpot Men who had a number one hit with Let's Go To San Francisco. They are still thriving on the cabaret circuit some twenty five years on from their heyday which produced hits like My Baby Loves Loving and Julie Do Ya Love Me. The band are led by Brian Johnson who was a singer with Vanity Fayre (Hitchin' A Ride) and Edison Lighthouse (Love Grows).

WHITFIELD, David

A former builder who became an international star in 1954 on the strength of his massive hit Cara Mia. The first male artist to receive a gold disc, Whitfield built himself a mansion near his Hull birthplace and continued to perform until his death in 1980.
Answer Me and Cara Mia (1953 and 1954).

WHO

Mod icons of the Sixties who developed into one of the most popular bands in the world. Twenty-five years of hit singles and albums together with ambitious projects like rock opera Tommy and Quadrophenia have ensured their place in rock history.

Drummer Keith Moon died of an overdose

Roger Daltrey now

The Who in 1960s

Pete Townshend now

of a drug prescribed to combat alcoholism (he died in the same Park Street apartment that Mama Cass of the Mamas & Papas died in four years earlier).

Roger Daltrey has a trout farm, Pete Townshend moves in the world of publishing and John Entwistle lives in a stately home in Somerset.

In 1996 the production of Tommy hit the West End stage, while The Who were joined by Zak Starkey, Ringo Starr's son, on drums. Following the trend for supergroup one-offs, they performed Quadraphenia in London's Hyde Park. The film of the same name was also re-released.

The stage show version of Quadrophenia toured the world in 1997 with Billy Idol playing Ace The Face and PJ Proby the Godfather.

My Generation (1965).

Marty Wilde

WILDE, Marty

Sixties rocker who managed six top ten hits including the UK version of Teenager In Love, Donna and Rubber Ball. In 1981 he returned to the pop scene as co-songwriter and producer for his daughter Kim's solo career. He still makes an occasional appearance on the nostalgia circuit and toured with old mate Joe Brown in 1996.

WILLIAMS, Danny

Found stardom as a fiteen year old with Moon River in 1961. He tasted chart success once more with Dancing Easy from the Martini TV commercia in 1977 and toured well into the Nineties. Since then. he has continued to make cabaret appearances and became a black belt in karate, becoming a top instructor.
Moon River (1961).

WILLIAMS, Mason

Well known songwriter whose credits include Cinderella Rockefella and then his own million seller with Classical Gas. Continued to perform and became a respected poet, author and artist who exhibited at Pasadena Art Museum.

WILSON, Jackie

Former boxer who survived being shot by a jealous lover. Died on 21st January 1984 in Mount Holly, New Jersey having spent nine years in a coma following a heart attack while performing on stage.

In 1987 Wilson's classic Reet Petite topped the UK chart thanks to an innovative animated video.
Reet Petite (1967).

WINGFIELD, Pete

From Liphook in Hampshire and best known for the high-pitched Eighteen With A Bullet (No. 7 in 1975). Became a producer with Dexys Midnight Runner, among others.

WIZZARD

Fronted by the evergreen Birmingham boy Roy Wood (ex-Move and ELO) the group's first five singles made the top ten, with See My Baby Jive and Angel Fingers reaching number one in 1973. Wood still performs live with the 11-piece Roy Wood Big

Roy Wizzard Wood

Band and now records for his own record label called Woody Recordings. Keith Smart (drums) is with the Rockin' Berries. Charile Grima (also drums) lives in London and is a part time teacher to blind children. Bill Hunt (keyboards) is a music teacher in Brum and still writes (with Dave Hill of Slade).
See My Baby Jive (1973).

WORLDS APART

One time teen idol and ex-boyfriend of Louise, Dan Bowyer left the group in 1995 to work in television. However, this proved to be a short-lived career and he now waits on tables at Croydon's Rockwell Diner while his former colleagues continue to wow large audiences, particularly in Japan and France.
Could It Be I'm Falling In Love (1994).

The Wurzels

WURZELS

The backing band to the late Adge Cutler have been performing their folksy music with a distinctive Somerset burr to the delight of their cider drinking audiences for twenty-five years. In 1976 they hit number one with the novelty record Combine Harvester, ironically a B side. The Wurzels now consist of Pete Budd who 'spends his spare time dangling his worm in the sea'; Tommy Banner, who has had to change his Grubby ways since getting married; Amos Morgan and Squire Wintour who used to play bass guitar for Neil Sedaka.

WYMAN, Bill

Playing for fun these days in line-ups of rock superstars, enjoying family life and overseeing his restaurant business. See the ROLLING STONES.

WYNTER, Mark

Born Terence Lewis in Woking and changed his name to become a Sixties heart-throb with songs such as Venus In Blue Jeans and Go Away Little Girl. Took to the West End Stage and has since appeared in Cats and Phantom Of The Opera.

XTC

Andy Partridge, Barrie Andrews, Terry Chambers (left 1982) and Colin Moulding hailed from Swindon. The mainstay, guitar and vocals were provided by Andy Partridge who went on to work as producer with Blur in 1992. XTC have not toured since 1982 but claim to be 'still writing'.
Senses Working Overtime (1982).

YARDBIRDS

In 1966 Eric Clapton joined John Mayall's Bluesbreakers and was replaced by Jeff Beck. Paul Samwell-Smith left the group to become

Thesps

Ten who have trod the boards

1. Adam Ant
   Funeral Games

2. Tony Orlando
   Barnum

3. Gary Glitter
   Quadraphenia

4. Peter Noone
   Pirates Of Penzance

5. Luke Goss & Craig McLachlan
   Grease

6. P.J. Proby
   Elvis & Quadraphenia

7. Cliff Richard & Gordon Giltrap
   Heathcliffe

8. Donny Osmond
   Jesus Christ Superstar

9. Suzi Quatro
   Tallulah Who?

10. David Cassidy
    Barnum

a record producer and later worked in the recording studio with Cat Stevens. Chris Dreja filled in on bass and Jimmy Page was brought in on guitar. The band responded but before long Jeff Beck parted company.

In July 1968 the group officially disbanded and Chris Dreja left the performing stage completely and became a successful photographer. Relf and McCarty worked as a duo before teaming up with Keith's sister, Jane, to form Renaissance in 1969.

After recording the album Renaissance the same year, Keith Relf left the group and worked briefly as a producer with Medicine Head. In May 1976 he died at his home in Hounslow when the guitar he was playing suddenly became live and electrocuted him.

Chris Drega and Jim McCarty took a new Yardbirds on tour to America in 1997, including Gypie Mayo from Doctor Feelgood. Jeff Beck became a guitar legend and retired for three years in the late Seventies, taking time to indulge in his passion for classic car restoration. After taking time out to buy and renovate a pub in East Sussex and to do some acting (The Pope Must Die) he is now working on some new material.

For Your Love (1964).

YAZOO

Alison Moyet and Vince Clarke parted company in 1983 but went on to greater individual success. Clarke formed the short-lived Assembly (Never Never reached No. 4 in 1983) then became one half of Erasure. Moyet's distinctive vocal style carved her a career as a solo singer.

Only You (1982).

YES

The original line up was Jon Anderson (vocals) Steve Howe (guitar), Chris Squire (bass), Bill Bruford (drums) and Tony Kaye (keyboard). Rick Wakeman replaced Kaye in 1971 as Yes enjoyed their purple period during the early Seventies. Wakeman left to pursue solo projects, had a heart attack then married model Nina Carter. Jon Anderson, following his exit, struck up a successful partnership with Vangelis.

The two gaps were filled by Trevor Horn and Geoff Downes who also charted under the name of Buggles with Video Killed the Radio Star. Downes has since released three

solo albums, been a member of Asia for 15 years and recently set up The Loco Recording Studio – where Oasis recorded part of their last album – in Wales with fellow band member John Payne.

Horn has devoted his time to production, working regularly with ZTT Records and with artists including Seal. However, in line with the current trend, four of the founder members (Bruford replaced by Alan White on drums) reformed in 1996 to release the album Keys To Ascension. Rick Wakeman only lasted a couple of months before leaving again.

YOUNG, Faron

American country star whose It's Four In The Morning climbed to number three in the British top twenty in 1972. He later worked as an executive with a talent agency before committing suicide by shooting himself on 10th December 1996.

YOUNG, Neil

Country and folksy rock singer songwriter who is working on an archive album – he has enough tracks 'to fill 32 CDs!' He has two sons with cerebral palsy and in 1995 became part owner of Lionel Trains Inc., a company that markets a device which allows children with the ailment to operate train sets

Heart Of Gold (1972).

ZAPPA, Frank

Guitarist and frontman who was acclaimed as one of the most interesting and bizarre artists to emerge from America's West Coast. Together with his Mothers Of Invention backing band Zappa produced over twenty albums before his death from cancer in December 1993. He was 52.

ZOMBIES

Colin Blunstone, Rod Argent, Hugh Grundy, Paul Atkinson, Paul Arnold and Chris White were part of the British invasion of America in the Sixties.

In 1969 the group split and Blunstone

Colin Blunstone of The Zombies

ZZ Top

became a successful soloist. In 1997 he resumed regular live performances for the first time in over 20 years and White and Argent become partners in production while the latter also founded successful Seventies rockers Argent (which included Hugh Grundy) and opened his own sheet music shop in London's Tin Pan Alley.

Paul Arnold (original bass player) became a doctor in Scotland, Paul Atkinson (guitar) was a computer programmer before becoming an A & R man and Hugh Grundy set up his own transport business.

She's Not There (1964).

ZZ TOP

Trade mark videos featuring leggy women and custom cars drenched in desert sunshine helped ZZ Top to a succession of British hits in 1983/4. They have continued to chart intermittently ever since and still tour in their own crazy style. Frank Beard (the one without a beard) lives at a ranch outside Houston called Beard World. He and his wife drive his and hers matching red Ferraris. He is also reported to have a remote control hot-tub, which he can switch on while on the way up the drive!

Gimme All Your Lovin' (1984).